Different Games, Different Rules

Different Games, Different Rules

Why Americans and Japanese Misunderstand Each Other

HARU YAMADA

WITH A FOREWORD BY
DEBORAH TANNEN

OXFORD
UNIVERSITY PRESS

OXFORD
UNIVERSITY PRESS

Oxford   New York
Auckland   Bangkok   Buenos Aires
Cape Town   Chennai   Dar es Salaam   Delhi   Hong Kong   Istanbul
Karachi   Kolkata   Kuala Lumpur   Madrid   Melbourne   Mexico City   Mumbai
Nairobi   São Paulo   Shanghai   Singapore   Taipei   Tokyo   Toronto

and an associated company in

Berlin

Copyright © 1997 by Haru Yamada

First published by Oxford University Press, Inc., 1997
198 Madison Avenue, New York, New York 10016

First issued as an Oxford University Press paperback, 2002

Oxford is a registered trademark of Oxford University Press

Library of Congress Cataloging-in-Publication Data
Yamada, Haru.
Different games, different rules: why Americans and Japanese misunderstand each other / Haru Yamada;
with a foreword by Deborah Tannen
p. cm. Includes bibliographical references and index.
ISBN-13 978-0-19-515485-6 (pbk.)
ISBN 0-19-509488-3 (cloth); ISBN 0-19-515485-1 (pbk.)
1. Business communication--Cross-cultural studies. 2. Business communication--United States.
3. Business communication--Japan. 4. Internal communication--Japan.
5. Intercultural communication--United States. I Title
HF5718.Y363 1997
302.2'0952--dc21   96-39554

9 10 8
Printed in the United States of America
on acid-free paper

PREFACE

On November 6, 1869, Rutgers and Princeton played each other in what came to be known as the first game of American football. The rules used were Rutgers's, and they allowed players to kick the ball, and to bat it with their hands, but not to throw or catch it. Rutgers won the game 6–4. When the teams met and played again two weeks later, they played by Princeton's rules which allowed for clean catches. Princeton won that game 8–0.

Communication works much like these early football games. Like the rules in American football, rules in communication spell out the criteria to evaluate a game: What counts as communication or the absence of it, what is good communication or bad, fair or unfair, lying or telling the truth. While rules give players a goal, strategic game plans demonstrate optimal ways of playing the game. Players draw up rules and game plans, then, to establish a measure for success and failure in communication, and to give themselves a reason to communicate.

Cross-cultural communication is the interaction of players from different games. Players of each game assume and expect the playout to go according to their own rules, but just as you can't play rugby with the rules of American football, you can't play in American communication with the rules of Japanese, or vice versa. If you do, the side that does not know the rules of the game in session loses out, as demonstrated in the early football games of Rutgers and Princeton. Of course communication is more complex than sports—the wins and losses, not nearly as clear cut. Still, in either game, success comes from experience in the games' rules, strategies, and actual play.

I had to learn this lesson about communication the hard way. Soon after I began to produce my first words in Japanese, I moved with my family to live in the United States. Three years later, I was back in Japan. While the three-year cycles across the Pacific continued, I fought my way through the labyrinth of American and Japanese communication by trial and error. Books on cross-cultural communication were either unavailable or too academic, and there was no one to tell me how to address many of the cross-cultural problems I was experiencing. All anyone could ever tell me was that there was a *communication gap*—a helpful phrase, if only someone could have told me why there was such a thing, and what we could do to try to close it.

In time I figured out a kind of definition for that catch-all phrase on my own. It went like this: Every now and then, the communication between two people with different backgrounds melts down into a thick gob of gibberish. In this definition, the gap was the unknown, and any attempt to clarify the mystery a futile and hopeless strain.

When I later looked for answers in the business world, I found myself empty-handed again. There, communication was a primary issue that got secondary attention: Currencies and financial instruments speak pretty much for themselves, they said. What communicators need to do in their spare time is to hone their "communication skills" to keep the machine up and running smoothly and tightly under control. At all cost, avoid breakdowns: They represent human error in an otherwise separate and efficient piece of machinery called "business."

As hard as I tried, I couldn't identify with either one of these popular metaphors. Of course I could see the manipulable aspect of communication that made it comparable to the efficiency of a machine, or its wondrous aspect that made it seem god-like. But when I spoke English or Japanese, I hardly felt like a machine that suffered sporadic breakdowns. Nor did I particularly see myself as a victim of an unidentified communication hazard.

It was only when I landed in a Ph.D. program in sociolinguistics in Washington, D.C. and met Deborah Tannen in her class on cross-cultural communication that I finally began to get some answers. Learning the theories of sociolinguistics and the technique of conversation analysis, I discovered a way to tackle cross-cultural issues and applied it in my doctoral dissertation, which compared conversations in American and Japanese bank meetings (Georgetown University, 1989). Revised and published as *American and Japanese Business Discourse* (Ablex, 1992), this study began my career in writing about American and Japanese communication.

Because mixing personal life into scholarly writings is an academic no-no, I tried to keep the lessons I had learned on my own out of my writings about American and Japanese business communication. But the harder I studied American and Japanese communication, the more the academic findings seemed to overlap with my private insights. I had stood in the shoes of the business people confused by incomprehensible responses. I had been stumped like the decision makers when the other side seemed to make unreasonable demands. Like them, I had often been angry and frustrated. And like them, I needed answers on how to manage two vastly different and competing systems of communication.

Backing my personal experiences with analysis, this book is an insider's guide to American and Japanese communication. It begins on the premise that Americans and Japanese misunderstand each other because they have different goals in communication. The American goal is to make messages negotiated between individuals explicit, while the Japanese goal is to keep messages implicit and assumed in the group. That each group has an idealized outcome for communication does not mean that Americans never engage in implicit communication, or Japanese, explicit; nor does it mean that Americans never explore group-centered communication, or that the Japanese never interact with each other as individuals. But by idealizing different aspects of language and relationship, and assigning contrastive weights to them, Americans and Japanese use and interpret communication in ways that are effective and make sense in their own group, but often get miscommunicated and confused across groups.

In chapter 2, I discuss key aspects of American English and Japanese grammar, or what I call "communication equipment." This discussion includes not only the mechanics of language, but what each symbolizes for Americans, and for Japanese, to show that even the most basic aspects of language reflect social beliefs.

In chapter 3, I shift from descriptions of goal-oriented behavior to strategy, and describe communication in use. Beginning with a contrastive definition of a speaker-based American strategy and a listener-based Japanese strategy, I describe some basic communication strategies, comparing American and Japanese conventions in naming, agreeing, disagreeing, thanking, and apologizing.

Chapter 4 examines the assumptions of American and Japanese business and the expectation of players in business communication. American business opts for a game plan in which individuals engineer their own projects, which they then verbally negotiate and ultimately record as written documents. In contrast, the preferred game plan in Japanese business is for a project to become collectively sanctioned through the grapevine, in a process often referred to as "consensus decision-making." The widely supported project is only then distributed across a team within which there are few, if any, self-contained jobs. By illustrating how business practices are founded on the same principles that govern other social interaction, this chapter underscores the frequently ignored reality that business is *part of* social interaction, not a separate, "technical" entity with special characteristics.

In chapters 5 to 8, I contrast American and Japanese business communication, drawing mostly from my ongoing research on the organization of American and Japanese talk in bank meetings. The comparison is by no means an exhaustive account of communication strategies in business, nor a list of dos and don'ts. Like teaching strategies in a game, it is neither possible nor useful to list each and every move. Rather, by giving concrete examples of how actual communicators play their game—how they open and close topics, distribute talk among meeting members, make points, tease, praise, and show listenership—I hope the examples will give both players and spectators a better feel for the game.

A comparison of American and Japanese role models follows. Here, I distinguish the American icon of the working man from the Japanese one of the nurturing mother, and examine how each ideal is represented in communication. I end this chapter on a discussion of how American and Japanese children learn (and parents teach) the values of their own group.

The last chapter is a critical examination of American English in the United States and the Japanese language in Japan. For both Americans and Japanese, language is a symbol of unity. English is the medium that bonds Americans of all backgrounds, so that together with citizenship, the ability to speak English is a key criteria for qualifying as an American. The same is true for the unity of the Japanese represented in the Japanese language. Language is one of the most powerful forms of membership, so that although it is unconscious, every time we open our mouths, we present ourselves as members of a particular language community.

Despite its advantage as a unifying force, speaking a particular language comes with a price because we learn the rules of one communication system, and become convinced of the reality enshrined in it. We then judge the world of communicators outside the system as illogical, because we neither understand their rules for interpretation, nor have the equipment or skills necessary to do so. To rationalize the mismatch between other systems and our own, we come up with negative stereotypes which we pass off as "understanding," for example that the Japanese are sneaky and evasive, or Americans loud and pushy.

To overcome the blind spots in our communication systems, we need to examine other systems not through the lenses of our own understanding, but through those of the insiders themselves. Otherwise, a Japanese communicator will always fall short of being an American communicator, and an American a Japanese. American and Japanese communicators are different from one another, and we need to compare that difference with insider information. After decades of trying to figure out Americans and Japanese, I have discovered that insider comparison is the optimal strategy for closing the communication gap.

Understanding American and Japanese communication cannot be achieved by a homogenized, "universal" perspective that sweeps differences under the rug. Differences are exactly what count—if American and Japanese meetings were carried out in the same way, or if trade talks were negotiated under the same assumptions, Americans and Japanese would come to the same conclusion about what went on. But that is not the typical outcome. Differences are what count because they create the potential for misunderstanding.

But just as it is important to understand differences, it is also important to appreciate that it is easy to equate difference with inequality. This is what often happens in the rhetoric of race and difference in the United States; difference becomes synonymous with inferiority. Likewise in Japan, a once popular idea that keeps coming back is the so-called westernization of Japan. Here, westernization is confused with modernization, so that to say that Japan is becoming westernized is really Japanese shorthand for, "We're as good as you are." Although "difference" can be interpreted to mean inequality, I distinguish between Americans and Japanese, and between American and Japanese communication, without meaning one group or one communication system is better than the other.

This brings to mind a final difference worth mentioning between Americans and Japanese. The claim that the Japanese are homogeneous is not altogether true because they do have ethnic minorities, namely Koreans, Chinese, Okinawans, and Ainu. But compared to ethnic minorities in the United States, the groups are proportionally much smaller. A comparison between Americans and Japanese is therefore between a relatively homogeneous group of people called "the Japanese" and a relatively diverse group of people called "Americans."

By and large, the Japanese and Americans whose communication I analyze are members of middle-class, mainstream communities. When I speak about Americans, I am mainly talking about European Americans with higher education. At the same time, because nonmainstream members often assume mainstream ideas and habits, the attributes I call "American" may also characterize non-European Americans with or without higher education. My guess is that many nonmainstream members share the views of the mainstream. My direct claims, however, are limited by my sample of European Americans with higher education and relatively prestigious jobs, like the bank executives I studied.

I close this preface with the point that every year, the United States and Japan lose billions of dollars on folding or waffling businesses. So much that as Copeland and Griggs report, up to half the people sent return home prematurely.[1] Worse still, with trade talks at its center, the United States and Japan are still pointing fingers at each other and calling each other names half a century after the Second World War. Mark Foster, a former special counsel to the U.S. embassy in Tokyo and currently a consultant to American companies trying to crack the Japanese market summarizes the growing resentment among Americans with respect to the Japanese trade deficit: "All across the country, people I talk to are looking at the Japanese as free-riders."[2] To this, the Japanese respond that they are merely an easy target—a scapegoat for all American ills. It is, in fact, the United States that has become a nation of lazy crybabies, they say.[3] All this time, and we still seem to blame and talk past each other.

A cynic might argue that nations need enemies, especially to compete. I disagree. While competition can mean rivalry, it does not have to mean antagonism. It does not have to lead to trade skirmishes, based on a stubborn refusal to make sense of each other's differences. Nor does it have to lead to a smug complacency, based on negative stereotypes that lead nowhere. Instead, with an understanding of cross-cultural differences, Americans and Japanese can challenge each other to achieve higher levels of competition and communication.

For this common goal of the Pacific Rim, I write this book.

ACKNOWLEDGMENTS

This book could not have been written without the help of a great many people. First and foremost, I thank Deborah Tannen, who found the time to read over my drafts—not once or twice but a dozen times, and with painstaking care. For the past decade, beginning with my Ph.D. dissertation left on the glider outside her home in Washington, D.C. to this current book, Dr. Tannen not only gave guidance on analysis and interpretation, but also provided specific comments on style and presentation. To my teacher, my inspiration, and my critical eye, thank you and thank you again. To Rebecca Oxford, Yamada Etsuko, Yamada Osamu, Okazaki Yohena Shoko, Clare Winslow, and Mike Mochizuki, who read this book in its various drafts and improved it with their comments and suggestions, I cannot thank you more.

I am also indebted to The University of Westminster for giving me the time and intellectual space to pursue my research and write this book. A special thanks to senior editor Cynthia Read at Oxford University Press for giving me the chance to share my work, and for her insightful comments and meticulous editing. Many thanks also to the staff at Oxford University Press for taking me through the workings of trade publishing, with particular thanks to production editor Kimberly Torre-Tasso and copy editor Neill Bogan. And, a thanks also for all those who purposefully or inadvertently became the subject of my study.

As always, I owe a great deal to my friends, who provided priceless emotional support during the writing of this book. And although words fall short, a big thanks to my family. To my husband, Bruno Mathieu, I couldn't have done it without you. To my son, Sébastien, for giving me a reason to finish the book. And to my parents, who gave me two worlds—one American and one Japanese—I dedicate this book.

CONTENTS

FOREWORD

I first met Haru Yamada in 1981 when she was a student in my Cross-Cultural Communication class at Georgetown University. Of the more than 50 students in that class, she stood out: I can still see her looking attentively from her seat at the rear right of the large classroom, and coming to my office to show me the article she had discovered that she felt described her. It was about "third culture kids"—young people who had been raised so completely in two cultures that they belonged exclusively to neither, in a sense to both, and in a larger sense to a "third culture" made up of individuals who spanned two cultures.

The daughter of Japanese parents who moved in three-year cycles between the United States and Japan in connection with her father's employment, Haru Yamada grew up in both countries. As a result, she sounds American when she speaks English, and she sounds Japanese when she speaks Japanese. Yet the impression that she is a "native speaker" of each language is actually misleading, because she harbors within herself a deep understanding of the other culture that the vast majority of native speakers lack.

In the years since that first meeting, I have gotten to know Haru Yamada better and better. She graduated from Georgetown University with a major in linguistics, then went on to do both master's and doctoral studies in our sociolinguistics program. At the end of her studies, she wrote her doctoral thesis under my direction, comparing Japanese and American business meetings.

Having spent her life moving between these two cultures and getting caught between them, and possessed of an inquisitive spirit as well as an observant eye, Haru Yamada found herself trying to understand the differences and similarities that were catching her up. She applied her professional expertise to a phenomenon that had personal as well as universal significance.

The desire to use academic training to shed light on one's own cross-cultural frustration is an impulse that has driven my own career as well. My doctoral thesis compared New York Jewish and California conversational styles—a culture clash I was experiencing as a New York Jew studying linguistics at the University of California, Berkeley. This became my first linguistics book. Later, the first book on conversational style that I wrote for a general audience, *That's Not What I Meant!*, began with the misunderstandings that I had experienced living with my first husband, who was Greek. These projects consumed me because I couldn't think of a topic more important than cross-cultural understanding. As the countries and economies of the world become more intimately interconnected, and as individuals move more freely between countries through travel and immigration, the need to understand how growing up in different cultures results in different ways of communication becomes more and more urgent.

But even those who will never travel to Japan, never do business with a Japanese company, and never talk to a person from that part of the world, will find the insights of this book illuminating and helpful, because the greatest benefit that comes of understanding another culture is a better and deeper understanding of one's own. This is parallel to the better understanding of one's own style that results from examining conversations between women and men, or between New Yorkers and Californians. I am often told by readers that they didn't realize there was any other way to say or do things than the way they said or did them. Their own ways of speaking seemed "only natural." But learning that others' ways of saying or doing the same thing could be so different, and yet have a logic of their own, they see that their own way of speaking is not "only natural" but rather represents a particular set of habits and assumptions. Realizing that there are other, equally natural ways of saying or doing the same thing gives them the option of trying out a new way, as well as the opportunity to avoid the frustration and misjudgement that results from cross-cultural misunderstanding.

If this is true for speakers of different subcultural groups—men and women, people from different parts of the country or different ethnic or regional backgrounds—imagine how illuminating it is to understand deeply the logic of those who grew up in an entirely different culture—speaking a different language, living in another part of the world. That is the great gift that Haru Yamada gives us in this book, and it is a gift she is ideally placed to give. Her own life has given her a rich source of cross-cultural encounters, and her ability to identify and deconstruct the telling scene, together with her linguistic training and research, have given her the means to unravel the tangled threads that create the cross-cultural knots she so deftly describes.

Through innumerable vivid examples, Dr. Yamada shows that the Japanese and Americans are playing different games, following different rules, yet judging each other by their own goals and rules. The result, frequently, is frustration and mutual misjudgement.

A particularly fascinating aspect of this book is that many of the patterns Dr. Yamada describes that distinguish Japanese and American communicative patterns are reminiscent of the gender-based patterns that tend to distinguish women and men in the American context alone. For example, Dr. Yamada tells us that many conversational patterns that typify the Japanese grow out of a focus on care, whereas contrasting ways of speaking that typify Americans grow out of a focus on action. Immediately one hears echoes of studies, influenced by the work of Carol Gilligan, showing that girls and women often operate on an "ethic of care," in contrast to boys and men. Another example is the expectation in Japanese conversation that a listener will utter far more vocalizations like "uhuh" and "yeah" than an American listener will. This parallels the finding that American women tend to offer more such listener-noise than do American men. Even the explanation and consequences are parallel. Many men, it has been shown, are inclined to say "yeah" when they agree, whereas many women emit a stream of "yeahs" to show they're listening and following. If it later emerges that an apparently-assenting woman really didn't agree at all, a man may feel misled—exactly the impression made on many Americans by a Japanese who was eagerly nodding and assenting in response to statements that he later turns out not to agree with at all.

Many of Dr. Yamada's insights are based on her original research on Japanese and American business meetings. One of her numerous observations is that the teasing she observed among American businessmen was a way of negotiating their relative status and power, whereas the teasing she noted among Japanese businessmen was a way of negotiating how relatively intimate their relationships were. Here again readers familiar with my work on gender and language (such as, for example, *You Just Don't Understand*), will hear echoes of patterns I described that tend to distinguish American women and men.

Seeing these and other parallel patterns yields the vital insight that the motivations and conventions that tend to be associated with women or men in a given culture are not absolutely tied to gender but rather are part of a wider system of motivations and conventions that can be differently apportioned in different cultures. In other words, the specifics that characterize one or another group within a given culture can vary considerably in a different culture: what we consider "masculine" and "feminine" can vary widely from what seem to reflect these qualities in another culture.

Especially challenging and fascinating to Americans interested in issues related to gender will be Yamada's chapter on the image of women in Japan. She shows that women in Japan cannot be facilely pressed into a Western mold of "oppression-subordination." The situation is far more complex and nuanced. Japan, she notes, is not bound by an ethic that sees worth in being paid for work, and consequently being financially independent. As a result, women who have traditionally not worked outside the home for pay are not seen as powerless for that reason. Individual worth in Japan is, in a larger and deeper sense, not a matter of independence at all; instead it is tied to the notion of *amae,* which has been translated as "dependence" but which Dr. Yamada aptly refers to as "sweet interdependence." In a system of *amae*—the model for Japanese relations in public as well as private, in business as well as in friendship—each individual has worth because of an interlocking set of relationships in which both individuals are dependent on each other. Strikingly, Dr. Yamada tells us, "In contrast to the working man in the United States, the national role model in Japan is the nurturing mother."

These are just a few of the ways that this book will not only help Americans and Japanese understand each other—and help anyone who engages in cross-cultural communication—but also make readers examine their own assumptions about themselves and about communication in the largest sense.

Deborah Tannen
Georgetown University

A FEW NOTES ON THE TEXT

1. To preserve anonymity, the majority of the names of people and organizations in the stories are pseudonyms.
2. Using the systems of reference customary in the United States and in Japan, I use first names for Americans, and last names for Japanese, except for children and friends. In referring to scholars and writers, I also use the customs of each country: First name and Last name for American and European authors; Last name and First name for Japanese and Chinese authors.
3. In referring to the generic third person singular, I alternate between using "he" and "she" in English.
4. The translations of Japanese into English are idiomatic except where a literal translation is necessary to show the original meaning. These are indicated in the text.
5. The style of romanization in Japanese is Hepburn.
   Here is a simple pronunciation guide of sounds that are often confusing for Americans:

- a   as in f*a*ther
- i   as in m*ee*t
- u   as in put
- e   as in f*e*d
- o   as in boat, but without the "w" sound which is a dipthong; dipthong sounds like "ow" in c*oa*t and "ay" in g*ay* don't exist in Japanese.
- r   as in te*dd*y where the tongue flaps against the roof of the mouth. The Japanese "r" sound is in between the English "r" sound and the hard "d" sound in Ted.
- A repeated vowel like "*aa*" is twice the length of the sound "*a*."
- Each vowel is pronounced separately, e.g., *ao* (blue) is pronounced, *a-o*
- Double consonants are "held" in a staccatoed sound.

Different Games,
Different Rules

◑

1

Two Stories, Two Games

One Sunday, I am sitting on the living room floor with my sister's two daughters in San Francisco, watching cartoons on T.V. On the screen there appears a crowd of ants, busily transporting food back and forth under the hot sun, and next to them in the fields are some grasshoppers happily chirping away. When the season starts to change, I recognize the story—it is none other than one of the famous Aesop's Fables, *The Grasshopper and the Ants*.

Funny, I think, in the story I remember the singers are cicadas rather than grasshoppers. Poor Aesop, the stories ascribed to him were only permanently recorded some two hundred years after the sixth century B.C., during which he purportedly lived as a slave on the Greek island of Samos. For the Japanese, another one thousand years would pass before the Jesuits brought the fables to their shores. As the story is handed down from generation to generation, it is not surprising that a grasshopper would become a cicada, or a cicada a grasshopper.

I continue to watch the cartoon version of the tale. The ants keep working on their winter store of grain, and the grasshoppers keep singing as the autumn leaves fall. Then, in a telling scene of snow, a lone grasshopper hops listlessly over to the ant mound. There, it calls down to the ants for some food.

One ant, bigger than the rest, steps out and asks the grasshopper what happened to his own store of food for the winter. The grasshopper says that it doesn't have a store because it was busy singing during the summer. To this, the ant responds: "Since you were so busy singing this summer, I guess you'll have to dance for your food this winter!" All the ants laugh, and the grasshopper goes off hungry.

At this point, my two nieces double over with laughter, not in the least bothered by the implication that the grasshopper will die from starvation. But I sit there stunned, not just because of the cruel lesson delivered in the fable, but also because I feel tricked. The ending of the story I remember is completely different.

In the version my grandmother read to me as a child, the ants invite the hungry cicadas in when they show up at their mound, and the story ends with the moral: "All summer long, the ants worked as hard as they could and the cicadas

3

sang with all their might. Now it was time for the ants and the cicadas to join to-gether in a winter feast."[1]

Two stories derived from the same source, but two entirely different alle-gories. Or were they? The American cartoon story shows the rewards for the hardworking ants, and the punishment for the grasshopper's laziness. The Japan-ese tale from my childhood memory illustrates the merits of both groups' efforts: The ants' hard work at storing food, and the cicadas' boisterous songs that cheered the ants on. Aesop can rest easy, then, because both stories commend hard work, which is thought to be the original moral of his story.

But a closer look shows that each story about hard work really teaches a dif-ferent lesson. The American story demonstrates the importance of fending for yourself. As the ant tells the grasshopper to go away, he says, "Tough luck for you if you fooled around all summer. Now you have to pay the price." The point of the American story is that each person is responsible for his or her own destiny. On the other hand, the Japanese story about hard work shows how everyone has a role in society, and encourages the idea of depending on each other in times of need. As my grandmother repeated the moral of the Cicadas and the Ants, it was as if she was telling me that the only way to make it through hard winters was to help others out and count on them for their support. The lesson in the Japanese story is that each person is responsible for everyone else. The two stories then, differ in the kind of relationships each endorses. The American story promotes independence, but the Japanese story, interdependence.

Each story is also told in different ways. In the American story about inde-pendence, the distinction between making it on your own and depending on someone else is sharp: life for the independent ant, hunger and probable death for the dependent grasshopper. In the Japanese story about interdependence, this contrast is muted since the cicadas' singing is seen as work and rewarded along-side the ants' work. The benefits of hard work are assumed, and the story fo-cusses on effort instead. It is because the cicadas tried their hardest, and sang with all their heart and soul—Isshookenmei, ganbatte, utatte kudasatta kara—that they were invited to share in a winter feast with the ants. The virtue of hard work is only implied through the veils of effort so that, like the black-clothed puppet masters who manipulate the Bunraku puppets in Japanese theater, the shadow of effort props up the theme of hard work in the Japanese story of the Cicadas and the Ants.

The contrast between the explicit message of independent hard work in the American story and the implicit message of interdependent effort-in–hard work in the Japanese story demonstrates the difference between American and Japan-ese communication. The goal in American communication is for each individual to speak up for him or herself, and to express messages in as explicit a manner as possible. In contrast, the goal in Japanese communication is for members of a group to depend on each other to talk about shared experiences, and to express messages in as implicit a style as possible. The key difference between American and Japanese communication is found in the delivery and interpretation of these explicit and implicit messages.

It may seem like stating the obvious to say that these differences in American and Japanese communication are the primary source of misunderstanding between the United States and Japan. But differences in communication have been overlooked, undervalued, and little understood mainly because, unlike a political event or the movement of market shares, communication is difficult to capture. But to ignore differences is to be lulled into the false assumption that we all communicate in the same way, only to discover that what we thought were like understandings of a trade conference, a business venture, or a political election were not so at all. We all have our own stories to tell.

The rest is a tale we know too well. Misunderstandings between Americans and Japanese lead to a growing mistrust. Deals are left dangling, cross-national partnerships go unventured, and corporate and political talks remain in permanent gridlock. No one really understands why the other side tells the story it does, in the way it does. The animosity between the U.S. and Japan deepens, and suspicions of intentional deception follow closely on its heels.

"That's not fair! They're not playing by the rules!" call out the opposing parties in mutual accusation.

To avoid these and other unwelcome misunderstandings, here are a few more stories about American and Japanese communicators, each with their own views on relationship and communication.

Strong Independence, Sweet Interdependence

A few years back in Washington, D.C., I was commissioned by my mother to find a house for my younger brother and two of his college mates, all three of whom were returning from their junior year abroad. On finding a place, I began calling parents to get permission to sign off on the lease. All was going well until I reached Mr. Brown, the last parent to give consent on behalf of his son. For reasons that were not immediately clear to me at the time, Mr. Brown hemmed and hawed on what seemed to be a straightforward matter of saying yes or no. Still more puzzling was that every time I asked Mr. Brown if he had any further questions, he reassured me to the contrary.

But when I asked, "So, I have your consent?" it would only bring on more hesitation. "Well, you see, my son, Gordon wants to know . . ." Mr. Brown would say, and I knew we were back to square one. I really began to empathize with the stories of Americans struggling to get a straight answer from the Japanese. Like them, I was getting nowhere. Why couldn't he just say yes?

Then, just as I was about to launch into another round, it finally dawned on me that I was asking the wrong question: I kept asking Mr. Brown for his consent instead of asking him to speak on behalf of his son, Gordon. No wonder each round of answers was prefaced with, "Gordon" this, and "Gordon" that. Gordon was a grown college student who made up his own mind, not a little boy who complied with his father's decisions. He was an independent individual who exercised his own right to make choices.

Realizing my mistake, I reframed the question and asked, "So do you think Gordon would want to sign off on the lease?" By recasting the decision maker as Gordon rather than his father, I hoped to stage him as the central player, with a voice of his own. That way, I thought, Mr. Brown could see himself as a speaker on behalf of his son who could secure housing for Gordon without denying him his due independence.

It worked. Almost miraculously, the gnarls of miscommunication seemed to come undone, and the new strategy delivered the answer I was after: Yes!

Replaying the conversation over in my head, I now see how my line of questioning assumed a Japanese orientation to relationships where interdependent members of a group choose a representative to express collective opinions and decisions made for the purpose of achieving a common goal. That goal, as articulated by the caretakers of my brother's future roommates, was to secure housing for their sons, and the appointed representative was me. Entrusted as the executor of a house hunt already sanctioned by a group of parents, I saw my main job as one of finding a suitable place for the college students to live. The rest, I thought, was just a question of going through the motions of getting parental endorsement on a done deal, and my signature in proxy on the pro-forma contract would only signal the official close of the house hunt.

But as parents of independent decision makers, the permission given on behalf of their sons was far from a mere formality. I later learned that the other two college students had already told their parents to say "yes" to the house. Each of these parents said something like, "He knows how difficult it is to find a house, so he's really happy that you found this place." The go-aheads that I got were, then, really the decisions that the students had made themselves and passed on through their parents.

Gordon, on the other hand, apparently finished his conversation with his father by saying, "Check out the situation and see what you think." His son's request had put Mr. Brown in a difficult position; I found out years later in a conversation with my brother that Gordon Brown was the only housemate who was paying rent out of his own pocket. Gordon's independence was thus not only social, but financial, and that made Mr. Brown's hesitation even more understandable. In a word, he wasn't in the position to give consent.

Reflected in my misunderstanding with Mr. Brown was a general difference in the assumptions that Americans and Japanese have about independent and interdependent relationships, respectively. As the anthropologist Wagatsuma Hiroshi said, "Americans are like peas on a plate, but Japanese, like rice in a bowl."[2] (The "rice" Wagatsuma refers to here is of course, Japanese rice that sticks together, not Uncle Ben's!)

More indirectly, this incident also shows how economics reflect social assumptions. American students paying their own way through school for example, demonstrate financially how Americans celebrate independence. Likewise, Japanese parents who provide financial support for their children exemplify financially the Japanese social preference for interdependence among group members.

What's more, cultural points of view both influence and result from our interaction and communication. For example, my experience of interdependence in Japan led me to assume that the parents' permission to sign off on the college students' lease was just a formality. But my quest for parental consent also produced an example of the Japanese concept of interdependence. Communication is a means through which we create who we are in relation to others so that American communication plays a part in constructing an American identity that values independence, while Japanese communication helps compose a Japanese identity that relies on interdependence.

Communication also presents us with an opportunity to endorse our ideals about relationship. By communicating in the independent mode, each American individual salutes an ideal: We stand up for our own rights, and look after ourselves. For example, we make our own decisions about housing. By communicating in the interdependent mode, Japanese group members pay tribute to their ideal: We blend in the common background of the hitonami (like others) and look after each other. For example, we make our decisions known to a decision-making center who takes care of us, and who we will take care of in the future. Writes the anthropologist Takie Sugiyama Lebra:

> In America, empathy is shown by giving Alter [the other] freedom to make up his own mind, while Japanese empathy [omoiyari] refers to anticipating and taking care of Alter's wants.[3]

We play out and create such different ideals about relationship because Americans and Japanese each have agendas of their own.

Mind Your Own Business

In one episode of the American sitcom *Blossom,* Blossom, the teenage daughter of a single father, becomes jealous of a woman her father is dating. In a stormy scene played out in the kitchen, Blossom tells the woman off, and forces her to leave. Later, she feels guilty and tells her brother what happened, but the audience anticipates a more important scene with the father, and this finally happens at the end of the show.

When her father walks into the living room and tells Blossom that he found out about what she did, Blossom first apologizes, then suggests calling the woman to patch things up. But the father explains that he is going through a process of dating, and that he has decided after all that this woman was not the one for him.

"Anyway," he says, pointing to the telephone in Blossom's hand. "You know what I'm going to say."

Blossom, relieved by her father's news, and by the appearance that he would forgive her, answers, "Yeah," and puts the phone back on the hook.

Then together they say: "Mind your own business!"

Screenplays tend to tell the ideal story, displaying characters in neat, organized representations. Here was one about the American ideal of the individual. "Mind your own business" means, "I am an individual with my own business to look after. I'll look after mine, and you look after yours." As an account executive I talked to jokingly said to his colleague, "Hey, this is my job, let me do it my way," the expectation is that each individual should do his or her own job, and not meddle in the affairs of others.

This ideal of independence is rehearsed every day in American talk shows where guests repeat with conviction: "I have to be my own person." Through variations on the American theme of self-actualization, the guests are really saying, "I have to find my own ways of doing things. I have to be independent." D. A. Benton urges this in her popular book, *Lions Don't Need to Roar: Using the Leadership Power of Presence to Stand Out*. Divided into three parts, "Stand Out," "Fit In," and "Move Ahead," the book ends with a discussion of the art of self-realization, which among other things is described as having the courage to do what others don't.[4]

Self-help books like this are examples of self-realization in themselves. Offering a kind of modern-day interpretation of the biblical injunction, "Seek and you shall receive," self-help books occupy shelf upon shelf in American bookstores reminding and encouraging Americans to live up to their ideal of the "bootstrapped" individual.

The antithesis of independence for Americans is powerless dependence. It is letting someone else run your life, a pathetic and fatalistic resignation to a situation that has gotten the best of you. Get a grip on reality, they say, because being dependent is being a loser. Writes Jerry Greenwald in a self-help book on relationships:

> Warning: Beware of the person who sends the message implicit or explicit, "I want someone to take care of me." Chances are he or she lacks inner intimacy and feelings of stability and self-love.[5]

The preference for independence in relationships is also reflected in American ideas about independent space and time. The expression, "I need my own space," for example, is formalized in a number of different ways in American households; getting your own room is one. In some families, getting a room of your own is a rite of passage, symbolizing a graduation from having to share your room with one or more siblings to becoming an adult with the privilege of private space.

The same independence is sought in saying, "I need time to myself." Like individual space, individual time defines autonomy in relationships, and autonomy—when no one tells you what to do—is seen as powerful. For instance, "I write my own hours," is a way of telling others that your job is a privileged one that is not circumscribed by others in time and space. It is short for, "I am in control."

But the privilege comes at a price because individual time and space are scarce. By controlling this desirable but limited resource—or some portion of it—you are preventing someone from doing the same. To prevent the undesirable outcome of vast inequality, American players accept a compromise agreement that might be called Equal Opportunity Independence: Every individual gets a fair chance, but everyone must honor others as individuals who operate under the same principle. A typical example of Equal Opportunity Independence is found in the dynamics of filling a job opening. Although everyone knows that only one person will get the job in the end, anyone can apply, and in theory, each individual is guaranteed a chance.

Equal Opportunity amends the American ideal of independence so that an American individual is not just someone who does everything she wants. She is someone who can play up her individuality, but not at the expense of robbing someone else's right to individuality. In *Blossom,* this conditional clause was invoked in "Mind your own business." If you want to be a model American, you cannot just step all over everyone. You have to read the fine print of Equal Opportunity Independence: Independence without undue cost to others.

Do As You Please!

If "Mind your own business" is a way of blowing the whistle on someone for stepping across the legitimate boundary of relationship, saying, "You're stepping on my toes, repressing my independence," "Do as you please!" is a similar phrase in Japanese. But here, instead of calling on the broken trust of individuality, the breach in saying, "Katte ni shiro!" (Do as you please) is in interdependence. A person who does as he pleases is one who is indicted as selfish: *Katte*. On the other hand, a person who indulges in the right amount of interdependence is commended as preserving the *wa*, the harmonious integration of the group.

Following the work of psychiatrist Doi Takeo, a number of psychologists, sociologists, and anthropologists have looked to the concept of *amae* (literally, sweetness) to explain the Japanese perception of interdependence. Defined originally by Doi as the reciprocal feeling of nurturing concern for and dependence on another, in practice, there is one interdependent who indulges himself in the amae (*amaeru*), and another interdependent who obliges (*amayakasu*).[6] In this idealized mutual interdependence of "sweetening" and "being sweetened," both interdependents benefit, and like a mother and a child, form an affectionate bond. In the long-term, the indulger and the indulged may reverse positions, like a mother who indulges her child early in life, and a child who indulges his mother later on.

But amae (sweetness) is not only restricted to the relationship between a mother and a child. It is pervasive in a variety of relationships in Japan, extending to any combination of sexes, and beyond what Americans might consider "personal" ones. Just as amae occurs between siblings at home, so it does too among men in the workplace. What's more, a person who knows how to look after others is commended as a *mendoomi ga ii hito* (a person who looks after others well), a quality highly sought after in managers, and a person who knows how to amaeru (count on someone) is usually well thought of and well cared for. In both directions, amae (sweetness) is considered desirable in the right amount.

But the balance is delicate, and the nurturer or the nurtured can upset the equilibrium in one of the following ways.

1. *Amayakashisugi*/Too Sweet: The nurturer is overindulgent, and spoils the babied.
2. *Wagamama*/Spoilt: The nurtured overindulges, and exhibits spoilt behavior.
3. *Tsumetai*/Cold: The nurturer is underindulgent, and does not adequately look after the babied.
4. *Katte*/Selfish: The nurtured underindulges, and does whatever he or she wants.

In Japanese relationships, someone who does not know how to be interdependent is considered too individualistic, and is classified in Category 4 as *katte* (selfish). Displaying so strong an individual character that he is thought of as *kosei ga tsuyoi* (literally, strong individuality), a person who always acts independently is often thought of as *hageshii*—fierce and hardened in character. The Japanese pity or scorn such a personality, concluding that the person has either been abandoned to the harshness of a dog-eat-dog world where no one looks after him, or has rejected the web of amae (sweetness) himself.

When a person who normally indulges in amae (sweetness) holds back, the Japanese call this aberrant behavior *mizukusai* (overly reserved) or *yosoyososhii* (acting like a stranger). I recently asked my aunt to bring over some dried foods from Japan, and then found myself mumbling about taking too much room in her suitcase. She laughed and said that was why I was so westernized; I was yosoyososhii. The message was that I didn't have to be so apologetic—I was her niece and I could have just assumed her amae (sweetness).

The reverse error of overindulging is committed by a person who is *zuuzuushii* (greedy) and asks for too much. To strike the balance between being yosoyososhii (acting like a stranger) and zuuzuushii (greedy) is best: Had I not made a fuss about the space in my aunt's suitcase, she most probably would have concluded that I was zuuzuushii.

When I explained the balance of amae to a class of American students, one member asked, "So you can't win?" In a way she was right. Amae (sweetness) is a fragile product of relationship that needs to be coddled and offset by *enryo* (restraint), making it as much a bind as it is a bond. For example, I have a reasonably personable relationship with my eye doctor, who also sells contact lenses. I can easily get contacts more cheaply elsewhere but I feel *warui* (literally, bad) not only because I know she counts on her contact sales to run her small practice, but also because of our relationship.

When amae (sweetness) is interpreted in terms of a Japanese understanding of time and space, it again illustrates a historical preference for interdependent sharing over individualized division. In traditional households, for example, rooms were neither function-specific nor assigned to individual family members, and this meant that the entire family ate, worked and slept together in one big room. Most urban Japanese homes today have western designs with rooms that are function-specific—a kitchen, a dining area, bedrooms, and so on—but relics of the past are still present, for example, when families with baths share a single bathtub, and families without them share baths in public bath houses.

Americans often understand what the Japanese think of as "sharing" communal space as a violation of an individual's right to personal space. My five-year-old niece, Sachiko, who grew up in California, expressed this vividly one summer when we were traveling in Japan. At first, Japan was everything she expected; her mother had told her about all of the things she encountered. Then one day, we went to take a bath at the *ryokan* (inn) where we were staying. Sliding open the door to the communal bath area, Sachiko's gaze was met by a woman, sitting on a stool, washing herself.

"Hey!" cried Sachiko pointing out the violation. "What's that woman doing in my bath!"

I explained to Sachiko that bathing, like other activities in Japan, was something the Japanese liked to do together, and she quickly recovered from her surprise. What I did not tell her was that communal bathing is an expression of interdependence among the Japanese that has its roots deep in Japan's religious history. The founding monk of Zen Buddhism, Doogen Zenji, teaches this interdependence in a classic quote:

A foolish person regards himself as another, a wise man regards others as himself.[7]

Taoist teachings also promoted interdependence. Taoism taught that because things exist relative to one another, a person cannot exist without others. Today, this Taoist notion of relative indeterminacy has given rise to a Japanese ethics that views moral and social standards as set by others.

In contrast to the American morality that calls on an individual to judge right from wrong against an absolute set of standards ("what I want to do is against the law"), Japanese behavior is constrained by others' point of view ("what will they say if I do this") that is reflected in the law. Good and bad is explicit in black and white terms for Americans, but for the Japanese, morality is an implicit consensus standard. It is this others-centered morality that drives the Japanese to want to be like others in the *hitonami* (literally, like other people), a desire Fujiwara Mariko describes as "keeping up with the Satohs."[8]

As the borrowed idiom suggests, the Japanese desire to be like others is like the American spirit of keeping up with the Joneses. But the American expression, usually meant as a negative description of material competition, is more like what the Japanese call, *miihaa* (the desire to be like Jane and Mary), and differs from the more general and pervasive sense of hitonami (received view) morality constructed on an others-centered ethics. Hitonami (like others) morality is what guides the Japanese in interdependence and ties them in conformity: "Deru kugi wa utareru" (Nails that stick out get hammered back in).

A Japanese mother, Kaeko, recently offered a lesson in this system of self-evaluation based on others' points of view. In trying to stop her two-year-old from making a face at me, instead of saying, "Don't make a face at Haru," Kaeko said, "Why are you making such a funny face? I bet Haru thinks you're a funny [odd] child. I'm sure she thinks you're funny." By telling her son that I would think he was an odd child if he continued to make a face at me, Kaeko was teaching her son to see himself from my point of view.

Confucian teachings also reinforced the principle of Others-Centered Interdependence. Says an ancient teaching:

> If one wants to establish oneself, one has to establish others. If one wants to reach perfection for oneself, one has to reach perfection for others.[9]

Expressions like *doozo* (after you) and *osaki ni* (sorry to have gone first) show how the Confucian principle of others first has become a ritual in ordinary Japanese interaction. Again, the concept of compassion and others first also exists in western societies as reflected in the common English expression, "After you." And Christianity also teaches empathy, often in the name of forgiveness. An American friend once jokingly told me that he heeded his father's advice: Think me first, me second, and if there is room for anybody else, me last. Of course the joke consists in the blatant selfishness of the advice. Had he no concept of considering others first, the remark would not have been funny.

But difference is a question of degree, and while the Judaeo-Christian tradition does teach empathy, it does not advocate putting others first at the expense of oneself. Acts ordinarily deemed wrong, like stealing, are considered acceptable if your own life is at stake. As with any joke, there is a kernel of truth in my friend's joke: Followers of the Judaeo-Christian tradition really do expect people to look after themselves first. The English dramatist John P. Webster, often quoted for inspiration in American publications, summarizes this point of view: "It is one of the most beautiful compensations of life that no man can sincerely try to help another without helping himself."[10]

As Confucian teaching contributed to the Japanese preference for interdependence, it also spelled out a more specific code of human relationship and conduct in which a key feature is the concept of the *bun* (a role). Literally meaning "a fraction," a bun is something whose member is not a whole person but a part of a group with the responsibility of taking care of others.[11] For example, an *oya-bun* is a parent-part who takes care of his subordinate *ko-bun,* or child-parts. The metaphor of *oya-ko kankei* (parent-child relations) connected in amae (sweet interdependence) is extensive throughout Japanese society, particularly in business, which I discuss in chapter 4. Briefly, in traditional Japan, a family ran a business; business was family, and family, business. During this time, the *ie* or house that ran the business was considered the smallest social unit composed of bun members.

Although the image of a family business in the feudal sense is gone, the structure it imposed on interdependent interaction has had long-lasting influences. For example, even today two Japanese interact on the basis of whether they are members of the same group, in which case the interaction is between *uchi* (inside) members, or different ones, in which case their interaction is between *soto* (outside) members. In interaction, say the scholars Namiki and Sethi, a Japanese always "establishes his point of reference not in terms of who he is but what group he belongs to."[12]

Not surprisingly, the difference between Japanese Others-Centered Interdependence and American Equal Opportunity Independence spells trouble in cross-cultural interaction. Americans living in Japan often find the expected amount of interdependence to be overpowering and infringing on their privacy. In homestays, young adults repeatedly complain about their lack of independence, which reportedly makes them feel like children. The Japanese American anthropologist Dorinne Kondo writes about her frustration in trying to adjust to the intensity of interdependence during her stay in Japan.[13] Once when she was sick, her neighbors continually check up on her, bringing her "get well" meals and other good will. But Kondo feels overcrowded, and wants to be left alone. As an American, the amount of amae (sweet interdependence) showered upon her was simply too much.

But equally problematic is the expectation of others-first gestures in a non-amae society where everyone is expected to look after themselves. In my early college days in the U.S. for example, I would go out to eat with some friends, and offer to pay at the end of the meal. In Japan, this produces a comical scene where everyone offers to pay, and the cashier or waiter ends up getting mauled with money. In the confines of a group of friends who habitually go out together, there is an unwritten rule that everyone eventually pays for one another over a period of time, but the charade is played out to show participation in others-first.

But in the pay-as-you-go plan among American university students, the assumption is not for a different person to pay for the group over a series of outings, but for the check to be split up evenly among the individuals at each outing. Money owed among American students is assessed immediately, not only because the resource is often hard-earned and scarce, but also because the relationship can be fleeting. Under such circumstances, it makes much more sense to settle accounts short term because if you wait for a treat to be returned, you might end up waiting forever (I speak from experience!) Also, the linguist Deborah Tannen points out that Americans may see someone who offers to pick up the check at a restaurant as flaunting her money instead of being generous.[14]

The Japanese intention of taking an American under their wing can feel to the American either like they are constantly in their overseer's shadow or being taken for a ride by a showoff with a hidden agenda. On the other hand, the American expectation that everyone look after themselves feels cold to the Japanese—like a superficial friendship which never reaches a satisfying level of trust. Understanding the American ideal of Equal Opportunity Independence and the Japanese ideal of Others-Centered Interdependence is critical in understanding how even good will can become twisted in cross-cultural misunderstanding. What's more, as the remainder of this chapter demonstrates, our ideals about relationship intersect with our ideals about communication so that in the combination of these hidden beliefs lie the answer to the power of communication: Communication both bonds those who share assumptions about communication and relationship, and sets apart those who do not.

Talking Guns, Stalking Swords

The popular western movie *The Magnificent Seven* appropriates the story line of the Japanese film *The Seven Samurai*.[15] The two stories are strikingly similar because in each, seven heroes are hired to defend a helpless farming village from constant bandit raids. But the stories are also different: In the Japanese movie, samurai defend a Japanese farming village with swords, whereas in the American movie, cowboys protect a Mexican farming village with guns. The different backdrops and equipment also set the stage for a key communicative difference; yelling swordsmen create unfocussed noise in the Japanese fight scenes, but gunmen negotiate the American fight scenes in verbal exchange.

Talk marks every confrontation in *The Magnificent Seven*. The first speaker is the villain Calvera, who comes to raid the village with his men. Mounting his horse, he punctuates his departure with comments to the village head, Sotero.

CALVERA: We'll have to have another discussion very soon. It's always a pleasure to hear the news of my good friend Sotero. Maybe when I come back, uh?

The scene depicts a brute thief slapping and ordering around a speechless farmer, and the story about a powerful-talking bully who uses unfair means to dominate the meek and silent begins.

When the villagers hire good guns to oust the foul-mouthed bully, Calvera, another exchange occurs, this time between Chris, the Magnificent leader, and Calvera.

CHRIS: Ride on.

CALVERA: You hear that Sotero? You hear what he said? Ride on! To me! You tell him to ride on before I become angry. Him. And others. Because if I leave here with empty hands, everybody will answer to me when I come back.

CHRIS: You won't come back.

CALVERA: Why not?

CHRIS: You won't have any guns. Take them off right now and drop 'em.

Then one day, the bandits trick the Magnificents into leaving the village. When they return, the Magnificents find the village occupied by Calvera and his men. As Chris and Calvera size each other up, they exchange a few more words.

CALVERA: You'll be dead all of you—if that's what you want.

CHRIS: Do we have a choice?

CALVERA: Of course. Sit down. Let's talk.

As Chris and Calvera sit down to talk, the opposing sides negotiate the terms of their next move. For here, in a communicative field where talk is honored, no matter who has the upper hand in the battle over the farming fields, or who is right and who is wrong, every respectable individual grants others the right to talk.

The law of talk that regulates fair play in *The Magnificent Seven* is completely absent in the original movie, *The Seven Samurai*. The first scene opens with the scuffle of farmers helplessly handing over bags of rice to the bandits in silence. Then, in each of the fight scenes where Calvera talks to Chris in *The Magnificent Seven,* samurai stalk the invaders through the farming village, and the fighting begins with noises of slashing swords and cries of battle. The fight scenes in *The Seven Samurai* are assumed without the discussions that take place before the imminent fight in *The Magnificent Seven*. The fights occur without verbal justification that they are engaged in "a fight."

The contrast between the use of talk by the American gunmen and the silence of the Japanese sword fighters reflects a distinction between views of talk and silence that again finds its source in the religions and folklore woven into the respective histories of the United States and Japan. Judaeo-Christian principles were in part responsible for spreading the present-day importance given to the spoken in the United States. Pointing to this origin is the New Testament verse, John (1:1): "In the beginning was the Word, and the Word was with God, and the Word was God. Equating words with God, John elevates speech to the utmost position of power and eminence.

By the eighteenth century, science competed with religion for prestige, and lexicographers of the English language began to see the deification of words as unacademic. Among the first to try to give words a man-made, scientific quality was Samuel Johnson. In the preface to his famous English dictionary, he writes: "I am not yet so lost in lexicography as to forget that words are daughters of the earth, and that things are the sons of heaven."

In a popular perspective on language that persists in the English-speaking world today, words, although backed by God, are viewed not as descended from the heavens, but created by man in a science of language. What was more, science implied exactness, so increasingly, it was not only speech that was important, but precise speech: By making the right choice of words, you can say exactly what you want. American law is a ritualized example of this view of language that seeks to assign specific meanings to words. In a courtroom where good and bad is determined in speech, ambiguity is seen as a flaw best avoided.

But in Japan, an entirely different picture developed from each of the three influential religions, Buddhism, Taoism, and Confucianism, together conducing to the belief that the unspoken is sacred. In Buddhism, for example, one of the major goals is to realize the emptiness of words. Kooan, the nonsense riddles of Zen Buddhist monks—like "What is the sound of one hand clapping?"—are meant to jolt a disciple into the enlightenment of emptiness.

Participants in Judaeo-Christian services do not always understand the language of the service they are attending, as in Catholic services in Latin, and Jewish services in Hebrew. The same is true for the Japanese who listen to Buddhist *okyoo,* a Japanese pronunciation and rendition of the sutras originally chanted in Sanskrit. But unlike the practitioners of Judaeo-Christian religions, whose aim is to understand a sermon in a service, Buddhist practitioners do not seek to understand or interpret the meaning in okyoo (sutras) because the point is to realize the emptiness of the chants. This contrast between the Judaeo-Christian and Buddhist viewpoints is probably what prompted my mother to look up at the domed ceiling of a Catholic church in Florence painted with cherubs and scenes of men and women in heaven and hell, and say, "I guess the idea is to *fill* your mind with sacred thoughts, not empty it."

A similar reverence for silence is found in Taoist teachings where forgetting language and remaining speechless is advocated as the ideal way (*tao*) to emptiness. The Confucian code of conduct, designed to guide group members through compatible relationships and smooth interaction, also discouraged straightforward speech because saying whatever you felt was seen as not always socially appropriate or graceful. From this convergence of religious ideas grew a view that explicit talk with definite meanings was often undesirable, and since talk always presents the opportunity to be overly explicit—that is, tactless and blunt—the

Japanese began to treat talk as a communicative medium that warrants caution and suspicion.

A long list of proverbs illustrates this Japanese skepticism towards talk. "Kuchi wa wazawai no moto" (The mouth is the source of calamity) for example, shows the Japanese fear of saying the wrong thing. Giving the saying an irreverent modern twist, the cartoonist Gomi Taro rewrites the proverb as: "Oshaberi wa kuchi no onara"; talkativeness is a mouth's fart.[16] Another proverb teaches the foolishness of talk: "Tori mo nakaneba utaremaji" (If the bird had not sung, it would not have been shot).

In the western world, on the other hand, speech was increasingly associated with the cultured, and silence viewed as the domain of the savage. Indeed, the French still use the word "sauvage" to mean "savage," but also "unsociable," someone who does not partake in the art of discourse. The anthropologist R. P. McDermott points out that American linguists have long interpreted the silence of Native Americans as failure to communicate, attributing it to savagery in early studies, and to the inability to operate in an English-speaking world in later ones.[17] Unlike the general population who looked down upon the silent savages, many anthropologists and linguists looked upon Native Americans as victims of the modern world. But either way, the ability to speak up signaled progress, while silence symbolized death, handicap, or the absence of civilization. A popular quote by Thomas Mann sums up this point of view.

> Speech is civilization itself. The word, even the most contradictory, preserves contact—it is silence which isolates.

Like the biblical saying, "Ask and you shall be heard," in the western world, the squeaky wheel gets the grease.

In contrast, the Japanese were only introduced to the concept of speech-giving in the late nineteenth century by the statesman Fukuzawa Yukichi, who took great interest in western forms of discourse and literature. Despite this introduction, the Japanese continued to evaluate halting speakers more positively, thinking of them as more honest than those who are too fluent. "Kuchi ni mitsu ari, hara ni ken ari," they said about these slick sweet-talkers. Honey in the mouth, a dagger in the belly.

According to this Japanese folklore of silence, only the belly speaks the truth. The best communication is without words in *haragei* (literally, belly art), silent communication. Such visceral communication is thought of as occurring between an ideal couple in Japan through *a-un no kokyuu* (literally, ah-hm breathing): If a husband says, "Ah," a wife would immediately understand, "Hm." Ideal communication is communication without talk.

Compare this to the statements of an American husband and wife team on *Donahue* discussed by the conversation analyst Donal Carbaugh.

Said the wife: The only thing that saved Craig and me is the communication. That's the only thing that helped us. The husband replied: I think that's the key, communication. The wife: If you don't talk it will never work.[18]

In the plethora of television and radio talk shows, audiences applaud those who talk. No matter if they have gone down the path of social ills, if they can say it, they can still make good. When you speak out on American television or radio, you are applauded for taking up the challenge of communicating through the American ideal of the spoken. Conversely, the same audience censures those who do not speak out; the silent, presumed guilty, are condemned. The American spoken indictment is sharp and clear, especially in contrast to the muted implications of talk among the Japanese.

Different Playing Fields

By exploring the American and Japanese perspectives on language and relationship, this chapter has drawn the lines in two different playing fields. The American field is one where individuals play out self-reliance and practice explicit communication. The Japanese field, on the other hand, is one where interdependent group members accommodate each other through implicit communication.

In each case, language and relationship can be seen as complementary. For the American ideal, saying something automatically singles you out, giving you an individual voice from among the group. By the same token, for the Japanese ideal, not saying anything and staying silent lets you stay undistinguished from others in the group.

The composite features of the different playing fields were illustrated in the two versions of Aesop's fable discussed at the beginning of the chapter. Recall that in the American version of "The Grasshopper and the Ants," a lone grasshopper limps over to the ant mound to ask for food, and a chief ant tells it to go dance for its own food. Talk occurs between two individuals.

In contrast, in the Japanese version of "The Cicadas and the Ants," there is no verbal exchange between the two groups of ants and cicadas. Leaving the potential exchange unspoken, each assumes the action of the other group, and their winter feast is described only by the narrator. The characters in the Japanese story then, assume an unstated interdependence, while the characters in the American story express their individuality by speaking up for themselves.

The message content also supports and expresses the biases of relationship in each field, and this is demonstrated in the different ways a scene is interpreted in *The Seven Samurai* and *The Magnificent Seven*. When one farmer begins to get cold feet in *The Seven Samurai,* a samurai recites the concept of war based on interdependence:

SAMURAI: Alright. That's what war is. Protect others to protect yourself. He who thinks only of himself also destroys himself. . . . Wars are not meant to be fought on your own.[19]

But unlike the Japanese war that is centered on organized units of farmers headed by samurai to fight against faceless villains, the battle as defined in *The Magnificent Seven* revolves around Chris's leadership as he says to the dissenting farmers:

CHRIS: Is that what you want? Answer me. Who is for going out? Who is for giving up? I want to know now. I'll tell you what I can do. I'll kill the first man who so much whispers a word about giving up. The very first man, so help me, I'll blow his head off.

By articulating his point of view, Chris not only shows his commitment to finish the job for which he has been hired, but also his dedication to play out the role of the hero: the individual who speaks his mind. Similarly, the Japanese defenders demonstrate their determination to stick it out together in interdependence by implicitly heeding the advice of the code of the samurai. In both *The Seven Samurai* and *The Magnificent Seven,* the communicators play to the boundaries of their own games.

But the integration of the two ideals in each composition is far from perfect. Our desires are seldom single-minded, and plural desires often compete with each other. This contest motivates a tension which the cybernetician and anthropologist Gregory Bateson calls a "double bind": An interactional paradox created by a person's conflicting needs.[20] Both Americans and Japanese must manage their double binds, but they are of different orders.

In American communication, a double bind occurs because the desire to attain independence competes with the need to be understood—a need that requires interdependence. This American dilemma is captured by an analogy introduced by the philosopher Schopenhauer, about porcupines enduring a cold winter. Deborah Tannen describes the double bind of the porcupines:

They huddle together for warmth, but their sharp quills prick each other, so they pull away. But they get cold. They have to keep adjusting their closeness and distance to keep from freezing and from getting pricked by their fellow porcupines—the source of both comfort and pain.[21]

The tension created by the double bind, or what the anthropologist Dorinne Kondo calls an "existential dilemma," calls for a balance between independence and rapport with others.[22] To cope with this dilemma, Americans systematically call on an amended target, which I called Equal Opportunity Independence: For a small cost that commits you and everyone to play by the rules, you can rest reasonably assured that your independence will be granted. The examples offered by

	American	Japanese
Summary of Communicative Games		
Goal	Explicit Communication	Implicit Communication
Communicative Field	American English	Japanese
Communicative Rule	Spoken Is Better than Implied	Implied Is Better than Spoken
Relationship Rule	Independence Is Stronger than Dependence	Interdependence Is Sweeter than Individuality
Power Axis	Spoken Independence	Unspoken Interdependence
Double Bind Axis	Relationship	Communication
Amended Goal	Equal Opportunity Independence in Talk	Others-Centered Interdependence in Talk-Distancing

Calvera in the "Let's Talk" scenes in the *Magnificent Seven* are verbal illustrations of Equal Opportunity Independence. By presenting himself as an individual speaker who honors the speaking status of his enemy, Calvera shows that despite his villain status, he is still obeying the rules of the field, both communicative and battle.

The confrontations in *The Seven Samurai* also illustrate the Japanese ideal for unspoken interdependence as the interrelated units fight their battles without explicit verbalization. But being silent and leaving things unsaid is not always possible in everyday communication; in fact, most instances of communication call for talk. To resolve their double bind, the Japanese distance talk by downplaying explicit verbalization.

In the following chapters, I describe some strategies the Japanese use to achieve this implicit and "distanced" talk. For example, a common Japanese strategy for distancing talk is to talk from an others-centered point of view. This is what the samurai does when he says: "Wars are not meant to be fought on your own." Unlike Chris, who centers the action around himself by using the first person "I" when he says, "I'll tell you what I can do. I'll kill the first man who so much whispers a word about giving up," the samurai forgoes the use of "I," and so minimizes himself as the person conveying those words.

For speakers of American English, passive constructions which avoid the first-person point of view are often considered not only bad style, but also evasive. Taking the evaluation one step further, some may even be tempted to call the samurai a coward with no point of view. But in a field where implicit communication is desirable, the contrary is true: Distancing talk allows the samurai to disperse the potentially divisive and harmful talk, and play up a code that binds the group instead.

As Americans and Japanese each strive to take on the double binds in their own playing fields, each takes on a different challenge. In trying to be individuals who speak out for themselves and at the same time do not silence others, Americans practice Equal Opportunity Independence through explicit communication. In endeavoring to be group members who ideally bond in silence, Japanese practice Others-Centered Interdependence through distanced and implicit communication. In striving to achieve their own goals in communication, each set of players executes fair play because, negotiated shootout or muted sword fight, each has a logic all its own.

2

Communication Equipment

Not long ago, a college friend, Mark, told me about a misunderstanding he had with a Japanese engineer he called "Masa" who worked for him. The two music engineers were talking about picking up some video tapes that were at their other studio. As Mark tells it, the conversation went like this.

MARK: How are we going to get the tapes back here?
MASA: I will go pick them up.
MARK: Oh, I thought Amanda was going to go because you couldn't go until tomorrow.
MASA: Yes.
MARK: So Amanda's going to pick them up.
MASA: Amanda is very busy. I will go pick them up.
MARK: But you can't go until tomorrow, right?
MASA: Yes.
　　　[silence]
MASA: I will go tomorrow.
MARK: [Laughing] But they have to be picked up today—in fact they probably should have been picked up yesterday.
　　　[silence]
MARK: So Amanda better go today.
MASA: O.K.

In this harmless miscommunication, Mark and Masa just seem to have different agendas. Foremost on Mark's mind is the immediate pick-up of the tapes. Checking twice on his understanding that Masa will not be able to go and pick them up until tomorrow, he suggests that Amanda, an engineer of similar rank to Masa, go in his place. But because Masa has seen Amanda put in a number of late nights in the previous week, his concern is about how busy Amanda is, and he presumably tries to take some pressure off Amanda by volunteering to go pick up the tapes himself. By looking out for his co-worker, Masa shows his *omoiyari* (empathy) and illustrates an example of Others-Centered Interdependence, while Mark practices a philosophy of to-each-his-own to demonstrate Equal Opportunity Independence, and to get the job done in a timely fashion. Both emphasize different priorities while trying to attain their own ideals of interaction.

But beneath the miscommunication of agendas is a more basic misunderstanding of structures of American English and Japanese, and in this particular example, between the forms of "yes" and "no." This is how it works.

In American English, "yes" and "no" require what grammarians call "agreement" in sentences: To be grammatical, a "yes" answer has to occur in an affirmative sentence, and a "no" answer, in a negative one. Applying this rule to answer Mark's question, "But you can't go until tomorrow, right?" would make the response either, "*Yes,* I *can* go today," or "*No,* I ca*n't* go until tomorrow." In practice, negative questions are tricky, and respondents usually flounder a little, saying for example, "No—yes, I can go today," or "Yes—no, that's right, I can't go until tomorrow." Such hesitations occur because a grammatical rule like agreement often contradicts a communicator's instinctive desire to be on the same wavelength with other communicators. In trying to establish a relationship with the people they are talking to while at the same time observing grammatical rules of English, American communicators end up saying "yes" as in "Yes, I agree with you," to the person they are talking to, and "no" to make the sentence grammatical, or vice versa.

This problem is absent in Japanese because the grammatical rule coincides with the interactional goal of maintaining a relationship, and communicators can forget about having to make the "logical agreement" in the sentence. A "yes" answer endorses what is being said, and a "no" answer contradicts it, so that grammatical responses to Mark's question, "But you can't go until tomorrow, right?" would be either, "Yes, I can't go until tomorrow (so I'll go tomorrow)," or "No, I can go today (so I'll go today)."

Both of Masa's "yes" answers to Mark's questions were, then, the opposite of what Mark thought he was saying. Masa's "yes" didn't mean "Yes, my plans have changed, I'll be able to go today after all," but "Yes, you're right that I can't go until tomorrow." Then, assuming that it was all right to go the next day, he added out loud that Amanda was busy, and confirmed that he would go in her place the following day.

What compounded the misunderstanding was Masa's single-word response, "Yes." Without clarification, "yes" in American English means the affirmative: "Yes, I can go today." What's more, because native speakers of American English know they get confused about answers to negative questions, they would have probably clarified their position even if they had made a grammatical mistake, saying something like, "Yes, I mean you're right—I can't go until tomorrow."

Complicating matters further was that Masa had also said "yes" to Mark's earlier statement, "I thought Amanda was going to go because you couldn't go until tomorrow." Mark interpreted Masa's "yes" to mean, "Yes, that's right. So Amanda is going today." But instead, Masa was agreeing with the second part of the sentence, saying, "Yes—it's true that I can't go until tomorrow," which only set up the miscommunication because "yes" without qualification in English means, "Yes, I can go today."

Although the misunderstanding between Mark and Masa was repaired before it got out of hand, it is easy to see how the difference in the logic of American and Japanese "yes" and "no" can lead down the well-worn path of negative stereotypes: Americans think of the Japanese as never really saying what they think, and the Japanese think of Americans as not paying enough attention to participants in communication. But such negative character attributions are useful only insofar as they show a lack of awareness in the underlying differences in grammar and vocabulary—the different equipment—of American and Japanese communication.

As part of the equipment of American English and Japanese, then, the words "yes" and "no" are examples of vocabulary, and the grammar is the logic behind the words, like the stitching on a baseball that holds the piece of equipment together. Stitches on a ball might be something a pitcher feels for when he throws the ball, but he probably doesn't think about how the stitches were made, or how they keep the pieces of leather on the ball together. Grammar works just like this. Apart from the few years in elementary school when we may have been coerced to learn parts of speech or recite conjugations, we don't normally have to think of the grammar we use when we are players in communication. But like the logic behind the "yes's" and "no's" that showed the source of the misunderstanding between Mark and Masa, an understanding of several key pieces of equipment in Japanese and American English can help uncover the essential components of the different games.

We Think, Therefore We Are

Among scholars of Japan, there is a running joke that says, if Descartes were born in Japan, he would have said, "*We* think, therefore *we* are." But if Descartes were really born in Japan, we would have to modify the quote further since the Japanese conception of thinking is more like what English speakers think of as "getting it," or like the English metaphorical "seeing" than the causal deduction of "If A, then B" of western logic. We see, we are?

But there is still one more adjustment we would have to make before the statement could really be Japanese: Drop the subject, "we." In Japanese, it is standard and grammatical not to use subjects like pronouns, nouns or names in sentences; the linguist Samuel Martin reports that about 74 percent of subjects are not articulated in Japanese.[1] Because not using a subject is the norm, using it gives it an emphasis roughly equivalent to stressing a subject in spoken English, or italicizing it in written English: *We* see, *we* are. So if we really wanted Descartes to be born in Japan then, he would have to say, "See, are," which is what a lot of Japanese looks like in literal translation.

Subjects in American English—pronouns, nouns or names—can be dropped too, but not without notice. It is neither standard nor grammatical to drop a subject, except the obligatory deletion of the second-person pronoun in a command or request, like "Please (you) think," where the (you) is dropped. For the rest of the time, if a subject such as a pronoun is dropped, it may be comprehensible, such as when the (I) is dropped in "Think so," but unlike in Japanese, it is a grammatical omission. Using a subject is the norm in American English, and dropping it is the variation.

As an instrument that maximizes independence in a game of individuals, American English requires the use of personal pronouns. Labeling two people as "I" and "you" for example, points out the distinction between two individuals. Nowhere is this better illustrated than in *The Magnificent Seven*. In rallying to the dissenters who want to give up the fight, Chris, the leader, uses the pronouns "I" and "you" to distinguish himself from the followers who must ultimately answer to him.

> CHRIS: [I]s that what **you** want? Answer **me**. **Who** is for going out? **Who** is for giving up? *I* want to know now.

In contrast, personal pronouns are not used in the same scene in *The Seven Samurai* where a samurai indirectly admonishes the dissenters for wanting to fight a disunited war. "Wars are not meant to be fought **on your own**" (or literally, by one person).

So here again is the intersection of relationship and language: The systematic use of pronouns creates the individual "I" and "You" in American English, whereas frequent nonuse of pronouns in Japanese blends the distinctions among individuals in the group. In American English, a specific person is explicitly defined by stated pronouns, but in Japanese, no one is singled out as pronouns are left unstated and implicit.

Another related piece of equipment in Japanese that blurs the distinction among individuals is the use of what I call "direction pronouns" in the place of personal pronouns. Direction pronouns are the terms of direction, kochira, sochira, and achira, which literally mean "this way," "that way" and a still further "that way," that are used as pronouns: Kochira (this way) stands for "I" and "we," sochira (that way) for "you," and achira (that way) for "he," "she," or "they."

In their literal sense, these terms are a softer and more vague variation of koko (here), soko (there), and asoko (a still further there). As direction pronouns, kochira, sochira, and achira are also softer alternatives for the literal pronouns—watashi (I), anata (you), kare (he), and kanojo (she)—pronouns which when used can often give the same impression as pointing to someone in English. As a kind of euphemism, the indefinite direction pronouns take away the uncomfortable sharpness brought about by pointing out individuals through the clearly labeled pronouns, "I" and "you."

Direction pronouns also play down the individual by not distinguishing between singular and plural. Kochira can mean "I" or "we," sochira can be either singular or plural "you," and achira can refer to "he," "she," or "they." Rather than highlight the individual by using explicit pronouns as in American communication, then, the direction pronouns blur the boundary between the singular person and the plural, and emphasize the spatial distance between vaguely defined groups in relationship instead.

So much for trying to make Descartes Japanese!

A Question of Timing

In a confidential letter sent by a middle manager in a Japanese company to a senior vice president of its American joint-venture firm, one sentence apparently gave rise to some friction between the two companies: "This [figure] meets our target as agreed in our 1994 contract."

The letter was written two days after an important meeting between the two companies in which the primary discussion was about whether the Japanese company could actually meet its target figures or not by the end of the year 1994. On receiving the letter, the senior vice president, Dean, was incensed at the idea that the Japanese manager could say that they were meeting the target figures as set out in their contract because the one thing he was sure about—and made clear in the meeting—was that the Japanese would not make the figures at the rate they were going.

"Who were they kidding?" said Dean in recalling the moment. "Did they really think we would forget the real target figures that were set out in our contract? Just after we discussed it in our meeting? We're not going to be the fall guys when our figures don't come up to where they should be."

Fortunately for Dean and the joint-venture, he didn't respond with an angry phone call or letter. Instead, he consulted a Japanese assistant vice president, Minako, who said she would try and scope out the situation by talking to some colleagues in the Japanese joint-ventureship. It all seemed to pay off when at the end of the day, Minako told Dean: "It seems that what Manager Shiraishi meant here, by saying, 'This [figure] meets our target as agreed in our 1994 contract,' is that it *will do so* (and he probably means hopefully) *by the end of the year.* I think the letter was just his way of saying they're sorry they haven't been doing better so far, and they'll try their best to gain ground now so they can fulfill their obligations."

Dean's antagonism lifted as he reread the first portion of the letter that contained an apology, and mentally replaced the word "meets" with "will meet" so that the correct sentence read: "The figure will meet our target as agreed in our 1994 contract."

The misunderstanding occurred because American English and Japanese encode time differently: English verbs divide time into *three*, past, present and future, but Japanese verbs divide time into *two*, past and ongoing present. Because Japanese verbs do not distinguish between the present and the future, the Japanese manager, Shiraishi, wrote "meets" when he meant "will meet." For him, the two forms of the verb were interchangeable.

But the misunderstanding that occurred between the two executives was more than just a simple mistake in verb tense. As part of a vast system for recording time in language, a verb tense is a man-made marker of time that allows people to remember what they did when. As the sociologist Norbert Elias says: "In a world without people or living beings of any kind there would be no time. There would be no clocks and no calendars."[2] Without people, there would be no need for other time-recording devices either, like verb tense.

Anthropologists and linguists have noted how different cultures track time differently. For example, the renowned linguistic anthropologist Benjamin Whorf wrote about how many Native Americans differed from their western counterparts in that they did not spatialize time, and impose on it a sense of linearity and progression.[3] Such different orientations to time are recorded in language to make vastly different views of time audible and perceptible in communication.

Americans and Japanese also have their own systems for dividing, organizing and recording time. Here is the premise of each. For the Japanese, the past, by definition is two things: It is shared, and the outcome is known, even if it can often be distorted. The further back we go, the more entangled our pasts—the more interdependent. Norbert Elias, in his essay on time, notes that some societies do not distinguish between individual actions if they occur in the past. "[A] man who says: 'When [I] built this house . . .' [may be] speaking of his grandfather."[4] Actions in the past are those that the Japanese can remember as interdependent.

In contrast to the established past, the present and future are changing, and the future in particular is unknown. This flux in the ongoing present requires communicators to manage their interdependence, so forming a category that is separate from the past. The Japanese see time as divisible by two: The known past of tested outcomes, and the unknown, ongoing present which requires thoughtful management of Others-Centered Interdependence.

The interpretation of time in European languages including English is presented along a different "scroll of progress" that unwinds from a future holding opportunities for individual claims on time. Time then scrolls back and marks off another segment for individuals in the present, which when established becomes an individual's contribution to history in the past. For example, a trader develops a successful portfolio by deciding on futures, trading in the present, and banking on the past. Similarly, a communicator of American English verbalizes these time segments to establish his credibility as an individual in the field of independence, and to mark off his achievement in socially recognized blocks of time.

Even though Dean and Shiraishi didn't know it at the time, then, their misunderstanding was not only caused by Shiraishi's misuse of a verb, but by a whole history of difference in the way Americans and Japanese record time.

Basic and Optional Equipment

Each game differs in the kind and amount of equipment it requires, and American and Japanese communication is no exception. American communication is equipment intensive in the basics, while Japanese communication is relatively light. The primary example of this is the sentence: An American sentence requires a subject, a verb and an object if the verb takes an object (a transitive verb), while a Japanese sentence only requires a verb. But Japanese has an abundant supply of optional equipment that linguists call "modality." As the name suggests, modality changes the mood or tone of a sentence, which depending on the piece of equipment and the degree to which it is used can change the meaning of the sentence altogether.

One optional piece of equipment the Japanese use often and in a different manner from their American counterparts is negation. There are two basic contrasts between the uses of negation in Japanese and in English. The first is that Japanese allows for multiple negations while English does not. The second difference is that the English negation "not" is front loaded *before* the verb that occurs in the middle of the sentence, while in Japanese negations are back loaded *after* the verb that occurs at the end of the sentence. The net effect is that in Japanese, a great deal of agreement and disagreement goes on towards the end of a sentence, while in English the agreement or disagreement is stated up front without change.

Here is an example of Japanese negation. In an extract taken from a meeting of Japanese section heads, the group is discussing the possibility of liaising with an American broker. At one point in the conversation, a section head named Yamashita sucks in some air, lowers his eyes, and says, "*Nnn*" ("Hmm.") Another section head, Fukuda, presumably picking up on Yamashita's tacit disagreement, asks, "Why?" Yamashita then tries to offer an explanation. But as the translated excerpt below shows, the tortured answer that piles on negation upon negation only brings on the group's laughter.

YAMASHITA: *Nnn.* (Hmm.)

FUKUDA: Why?

YAMASHITA: → Well, uhhm, I would **not** say I wouldn't say that it's **not** that you know, it's definitely **out of the question.** So, in other words, I want to say that it is **not** that it wouldn't happen. I couldn't say ⌈that. [Laugh]

FUKUDA: ⌊[Laughing] What's that? You yourself . . . [are even ⌈laughing at your own torturous sentences.]

KANDA: ⌊[Laughing] No way. What . . . That's a big minus for you, Yamashita-san [Mr. Yamashita]. It would be really bad if you did something like that [in a meeting with Americans]. [Laugh]

The group, in tears from laughing by this time, is amused not only by Yamashita's reluctance to spit out what he meant, but also by his abuse of the Japanese equipment of negation.

Unlike English, where the negation "not" is required before the verb, as in, "I do *not* like you," in Japanese, the negation "nai" (not) comes after the verb that comes at the end of the sentence. A literal translation of, *Soo de wa nai,* would come out as, "So not" (not so). Because the negative nai is backloaded at the end of the verb which is at the end of the sentence, Japanese speakers can wait until the last moment to decide whether they are going to affirm or negate their position.

Such equipment is particularly useful in watching the reactions of others before committing to a position. You can start out a sentence in disagreement, for example, and then change tack and agree. Or, much the way the teasing tag, "*Not*" is added in American English after goading someone into believing something that was said, you can start off by agreeing, and then show that you really disagree. Yamashita went back and forth doing both in the span of a few seconds.

But as tortured as it sounded to his colleagues, Yamashita was not officially violating any rules of play in Japanese communication because Japanese grammar allows for double negation. A double negation like, "It's *not* that I *don't* like you," or even, a triple negation like "I wouldn't not say that I don't like you" is grammatical. There is no grammatical limit for negation—only the restriction of comprehension.

This is not at all true in English where double negatives are ungrammatical, frowned upon, and used to confuse people. Like a prosecutor's leading question, "Is it *not* the case that you were not in the vicinity of . . ." it is a line of questioning that quickly gets called out-of-bounds in a courtroom, receives a thumbs down in ethics, and generally arouses suspicion. A widely held view among English speakers is that double negatives (like those that occur in other European languages) are illogical because two negatives cancel each other out. This received view owes itself to a quirky pronouncement made in the mid-1700s by Bishop Robert Lowth of London, who had particular likes and dislikes in the English language, double negatives being one of his dislikes.[5] As a result, double negatives have since been ruled incorrect—as not altogether "legal" in the communicative field of English.

Not so in the field of Japanese. On purely technical grounds, Yamashita's two sentences, each with triple negatives, are grammatical. In addition, on social grounds, multiple negation is a vital piece of equipment in a field where Others-Centered Interdependence is the goal, because monitoring the reactions of the person you are talking to by making careful adjustments to the end of a verb allows you to best consider their feelings. Yamashita was presumably trying to do this by disagreeing without explicitly disapproving the others' contradictory opinions.

But everything has its limits. And as Yamashita's laughter joining Fukuda's and Kanda's showed, even he knew he overdid it.

Verbs That Give Up

One day in the spring of 1994, I found two consecutive messages on my answering machine. Both were Japanese graduate students who promised to call back later. But the first one said, "Mata odenwa itashimasu," or, "(I) will call again," while the second one said, "Mata odenwa sashiagemasu," or, "(I) will call (you) again."

The sentences come out roughly the same in English translation, and even in Japanese, the first two words are identical; *mata* means "again," and *odenwa* means "telephone call." The callers do not name themselves with a pronoun, nor do they refer to me with one. The only words that are different in Japanese are *itashimasu*, "do," and *sashiagemasu*, "give." The distinction between the two verbs reflects more than a different choice of words. It is a peek into the entire system of Japanese verbs categorized according to the relationship of speaker and other.

In contrast to American English, Japanese does not conjugate verbs according to person so that whether the subject is "I," "you," "s/he/it," "we," or "they" the verb ending is always the same. Instead of verb endings that emphasize the individuals represented in each of these pronouns, Japanese have verb endings that emphasize relationship; verbs that show the irreducible relation of speaker to hearer.

As with speakers of American English, the Japanese change the way they talk depending on the person they are talking to. If they are friends, their speech is more casual, if not, their speech is more formal. So for both Americans and Japanese, the principle that the style of communication changes according to the type of relationship is the same. Only in Japanese, the friendly/not-so-friendly criteria is only the beginning.

The second cut comes in the "not-so-friendly" category where the question to ask about the relationship is: Are we on an even footing in social or professional standing? The answer determines the verb form. If the answer is "yes," the verb form is neutral. If the answer is "no," two systems of verb forms go into simultaneous operation: Respectful form in verbs that refer to your audience, and humble form for verbs that refer to yourself.

Take for example, the verb "give" (as in "give" a phone call). In the not-so-friendly category, the verb "give" for someone on even footing is *agemasu* (neutral form). In the category of uneven footing, "give" is *sashiagemasu* (respectful form) to refer to the higher-up, and "doing the giving to the higher-up" is *itashimasu* (humble form) to refer to yourself.

So back to the graduate students who each said, "I'll give you a phone call," both chose the not-so-friendly and uneven footing category. But while the first student used the humble form *itashimasu* to refer to *herself* making the call, the second student used the respectful form *sashiagemasu* to refer to making the call to me. In other words, the first sentence emphasizes the lower status of the speaker, while the second emphasizes the higher status of the hearer.

It is because the verbs reflect *who* is being referred to that, as a listener, I was able to insert the implicit pronouns. In the first sentence, *itashimasu* in the humble form points to the unmentioned pronoun "I." In the second sentence, the verb *sashiagemasu* in the respectful form implies the unsaid pronoun "I," but points to the unsaid pronoun "you." So like the variety available for different kinds of golf clubs, there is sometimes a choice among equipment in communication. The two students chose from among these to achieve the common task of giving respect up the ladder.

Close and Yet So Uneven

If students talk *up* to their professors using the respectful form to refer to them, and the humble form to refer to themselves, do the professors talk *down* to their students? The simple answer is they can talk down because such a level of speech exists. In theory, social or professional "higher ups" talk down to those lower in status. Logically, this represents a true hierarchy that stipulates something like: Employee talks up to higher-status Boss, and Boss talks down to lower-status Employee.

But the equation for hierarchy is less symmetrical in practice, and many bosses use the neutral form with their employees. There are three reasons for this asymmetry. First, there is some evidence that lower-status form like yarimasu for "give" are becoming more restricted in use. *Yarimasu* (give), traditionally used in giving to lower-status members of a family or business is increasingly used today to refer to giving to nonhumans, such as in giving food to animals, or water to plants. Other people use the neutral form *agemasu* (give) unilaterally, and almost never use yarimasu (give) at all.[6]

The second reason is the others-first principle as applied to speech. Thinking of the other means raising the other person to a higher status by using the respectful form, while lowering one's own position with the humble form. If everyone does this, it becomes like a typical comedy at a restaurant, except that instead of everyone scrambling to the cashier to try to pay for lunch, everyone tries to "raise up" the other person while lowering themselves.

The final reason why talking *up* is not often returned with talking down has to do with the dynamics of *amae* (expectation of interdependence) in speech: Because amae is the careful balance of closeness in a hierarchical relationship, speech that reflects it is not static. Rather, the language of amae between two people of uneven footing is more like a game where players have to keep a magnet from touching a steel circle around it: The goal of keeping the magnet from touching the edges is often accompanied by erratic moves by the players. The game is neither completely symmetrical or even.

But as Deborah Tannen points out, because Americans assume hierarchy and closeness are mutually exclusive, they are confused by the way Japanese language encodes hierarchical relationships.[7] I had a student who once asked, "So it's not like one guy is doing all the groveling, and the other guy is doing all the shouting and ordering around, then?" Not quite. Amae (sweetness in interdependence) is about hierarchy, but it is also about closeness, because Japanese hierarchy does not preclude closeness. Even in the seemingly severest of hierarchies, amae can be discovered underneath. If there is no amae, then it is a cold hierarchial relationship, and one that would not be highly esteemed by the Japanese. The thing to remember in Japanese is that hierarchy is not the opposite of close: It just means uneven.

Order of Play

One final difference between English and Japanese worth mentioning is the degree to which order of equipment affects meaning. Like bases numbered in ascending order in the baseball field, in an English sentence each piece of equipment comes in a specific order of play: Subject (S), verb (V), and object (O). That order of play affects meaning so that the sentence, "I (S) ate (V) the shark (O)" in which "I" am the subject and "the shark" is the object is different from, "The shark (S) ate (V) me (O)," in which the subject and the object are reversed. Word order has meaning in English.

Japanese, on the other hand, has what linguists call "particles" that follow each word and identify their part of speech, making meaning less dependent on word order. The formal word order in a Japanese sentence is, Subject (S), Object (O), Verb (V), where the verb comes at the end. But if the subject and object are used, they can be switched without affecting meaning. In other words there is no difference between the sentences, "I (S) shark (O) ate (V)," and "Shark (O) I (S) ate (V)," as long as "I" is always followed by the subject particle, and "shark" with the object particle.

The relatively fixed word order in English versus the flexible order in Japanese has an important effect on how communicators express emphasis in speech. Because parts of speech can be moved around in a Japanese sentence, Japanese speakers tend to emphasize a word by putting it in the beginning of a sentence. In contrast, because the position of parts of speech are more fixed in English, English speakers emphasize a word by stressing it. Japanese speakers also use

Summary of Communication Equipment		
	American Communication	Japanese Communication
Sentence Order Obligatory Parts	Subject(S) + Verb(V) + Object(O) (S) + (V) + (O) If Verb Is Transitive (Takes Object) (S) + (V) If Verb Is Intransitive	Subject(S) + Object(O) + Verb(V) (V) Only
Standard Pronoun Usage	Usage Required Deletion of Second Person Pronoun "You" Only in Command Form	Usage Optional Frequent Deletion
Alternative Pronouns	None	Numerous e.g., Direction Pronouns
Time in Tenses	Past, Present, Future	Past and Ongoing Present
Position of Negation	Frontloaded Before Verb	Backloaded After Verb
Number of Grammatical Negations	One	Zero Grammatical Limit Comprehensibility Limit Only
Key Verb Distinction	Between Individuals as in Conjucation	Between Members of a Group as in Hierarchical Verb Forms
Emphasis	Stress	Word Position (at the Beginning of the Sentence)

stress for emphasis, but as a rule, Japanese emphasis is found in word order, while American emphasis is shown through intonation.

In cross-cultural communication, missing a point of emphasis can mean missing a point altogether. In his study of British–East Indian interaction, anthropologist John Gumperz shows how a large part of the British stereotype of East Indians as "rude" owes itself to the East Indians' non-British use of stress and intonation.[8] For example, native British waitresses used rising intonation when serving gravy, and said, "Gravy?" whereas Indian waitresses used falling intonation and said, "Gravy." The same word with a rising intonation was heard by British customers as, "Would you like some gravy?" but with a falling intonation was heard as, "Take it or leave it. This is gravy." In the same manner, stereotypes about Americans and Japanese emerge from their mutual inability to understand their different grammars of emphasis. Unexpected uses of stress often end up creating the stereotype that the Japanese are monotonic, reserved and cold, while Americans are overly emotional and aggressive.

Different systems of emphasis, like the other eight pieces of equipment discussed in this chapter and summarized in the table, are part of the equipment that make up American English and Japanese. But equipment is only as good as its users and their ability to use them. So that's the topic of chapter 3: players and their use of some standard strategies in American and Japanese communication.

3

Speak for Yourself,
Listen to Others

I have a Japanese friend, Chie, who constantly completes other people's sentences. You might know someone like this too, but in Japanese, people do this all the time—but usually not out loud. Being able to guess at what others are going to say is central to the Japanese expectation of unspoken interdependence: Like a person who is only a *bun,* or part of a larger group, a sentence in Japanese is only part of the larger interaction, and consequently often gets completed *across* communicators rather than by a single individual on her own.

The process of anticipatory guesswork required to fill out each other's communication is called *sasshi,* a strategy where players try to understand as much as possible from the little that is said. A sasshi no ii hito (literally, a person with good sasshi) is someone who is quick to understand and empathize, and a sasshi no tsuku hito (literally, a person who can hit on sasshi) is one who is perceptive. Both are people who can "hear others out" with little need for explanation.

In practice, the way sasshi works is similar to the assumption that goes into asking, "Guess what?" Most of the time, the speaker has a pretty good idea that the listener can guess the answer. A person who is good at sasshi is then, a person who can fill in the blanks without having to ask, "What?"

The sociologist Douglas Maynard analyzes a similar communication strategy used by American doctors and counselors. Called "perspective display," it's a strategy where doctors apparently let the patient or the patient's guardian say what they think is the problem. Because patients usually have some idea of their ailment, their perspective display allows doctors to position their comment and soften the delivery of their diagnosis.[1]

Sasshi (guesswork) is honed in the context of people who have known each other for a long time. Take for example, two Japanese bank executives, Igarashi and Maeda, who have spent some thirty-odd years working together. In one meeting, Igarashi asks Maeda to comment on a proposal. Maeda responds only with: "Sore wa chotto . . ." which means, "That's a little . . ." But Igarashi, sensing Maeda's reluctance to comment, immediately guesses that Maeda disagrees with the proposal. In a later meeting, he tells another colleague about Maeda's negative position, and even goes on to infer why Maeda disagreed. The probability that Igarashi would "guess right" was relatively high given that the two men had worked together in the same company for so long. Still, Igarashi's guesswork is noteworthy since Maeda's position on the proposal was only represented by "Sore wa chotto . . ." (That's a little . . .).

A more recent example of sasshi (guesswork) came up when I called my friend in Washington, D.C. to find out how her parents were after the earthquake in Kobe in 1995. Here is the beginning of the conversation.

ME:	Moshi moshi.	Hello?
MAYA:	N. Daijoobu datta.	Yeah, they were O.K.
	Arigatoo.	Thanks (for worrying).

Maya's use of sasshi was instant, and all she needed to answer the unasked question was the sound of my voice.

The use of sasshi is also well documented in Okazaki Yohena Shoko's study of husband-wife conversations. In an interview with Okazaki, a Japanese man named Satoru distinguishes the intelligent person who is good at sasshi from the stupid one to whom everything has to be clearly spelled out. Okazaki reports:

> If he has to tell everything in order to be understood, he feels like he is talking to a "dumb" person, or baka-na hito in his words. An intelligent conversationalist, he says, should be able to infer what a partner is saying without hearing every word.[2]

Like Satoru, Japanese think of listeners who actively participate in sasshi as good communicators, and those who do not as bad ones. For the Japanese, the responsibility of communication rests with the audience, making listener interpretation not only key, but the main mode of communication.

In contrast, an American consultant Roy describes a good communicator as "an articulate person who gets his points across quickly and clearly," and a bad one as someone who "mumbles and hesitates—people who just can't get their ideas across." This idea can be found in innumerable self-help books on business and communication, and in theories of communication and interaction in linguistics, communication theory and sociology. Authors in all of these disciplines characterize the speaker as creating (and controlling) meaning, referring to the audience only secondarily or not at all. For the American player, then, the responsibility for communication rests with the speaker.

Contrasting the listener-based mode of Japanese communication with the speaker-centered American one, I will call Japanese communicative strategies Listener Talk, and American ones, Speaker Talk. Both are active and involved modes of communication. A person who practices Listener Talk does not "zone out" while a speaker is talking, just as a person who practices Speaker Talk does not speak into a vacuum.

In the following exchange between an American consultant, Brian, and a Japanese bank executive, Kamiya, Brian is selling a proposal to Kamiya which entails giving cash incentives to executives who increase the bank's profitability. Both professionals participate actively in clarifying their mutual understanding. But in asking, "You understand what **I mean?**" Brian conveys his thoughts on what he means as a *speaker,* and in beginning his response with, "**You're saying** . . . ,"" Kamiya checks his interpretation as a *listener.*

> BRIAN: You understand what **I mean?**
> KAMIYA: **You're saying** that we should ignore this year in our calculations.

Then, in trying to sell his proposal further, Brian emphasizes his authority as a speaker as he conveys the benefits of the incentive plan.

> BRIAN: Once you're there [at an increased level of profitability], maintaining a 14 or 15 percent return on equity—14 essentially—and **I really mean this, I'm not just saying this, I mean based on my experience,** it would triple and quadruple the value of the bank.

In both of the above examples, Brian pursues his goal for clear delivery by clarifying speaker meaning represented in the pronoun "I."

As Brian sells his plan, Kamiya interprets them by echoing his understanding. For example, when Brian corrects Kamiya's earlier misinterpretation that the maximum sum to be paid out (a set figure) does not equal the target sum (a figure to be determined by the CEO), Kamiya reinterprets what Brian is saying through Listener Talk.

> BRIAN: That's not what I meant there.
> KAMIYA: I see.
> BRIAN: That's one reason why I wanted to talk.
> KAMIYA: → So you have this five-year period, to build from a 5.5 to 14. And then **you're saying,** from achieving from 5.5—even though 14 is just an average, because we're so below market, average, that to get there is extraordinary, right? But **your point is,** so, therefore people deserve extraordinary payments. High bonuses.

As Kamiya checks his own understanding, he uses the pronoun "you" to restate what the speaker says, and pursues his goal of interpretation in Listener Talk.

In the exchange above, Brian is the seller, and Kamiya, the buyer, so from a business point of view it is Brian's primary goal to convey his ideas, and Kamiya's primary goal to understand them. But American communicators use Speaker Talk, and Japanese, Listener Talk, even when the American communicator is principally the listener (buyer), and the Japanese communicator principally the speaker (seller). For example, in Douglas Maynard's study of doctor-patient communication, the listening patient (buyer) uses perspective display as an opportunity to speak up for herself. Likewise, sasshi illustrates the continuous guesswork done by the speaker who must constantly monitor the effect of his words on his audience. The mode of communication that Americans seek and vie for, then, is the position of the speaker, while the mode of communication that the Japanese seek to achieve is that of the listening audience.

The playout between American Speaker Talk and Japanese Listener Talk gives rise to mutual accusations in cross-cultural interaction ranging from comical to caustic. On the humorous end is a conversation that took place between Chie and another American friend, Fiona. As usual, Chie was verbalizing her sasshi (guesswork) in English, and completing Fiona's sentences. Fiona caught on to this after a while, and began speaking faster so she could finish her sentences on her own. But the faster she spoke, the more Chie tried to show her empathy, supplying sentence-endings with unmatched speed. "I'm listening, see, I can even complete your thoughts," I suppose, was the message she was trying to convey.

But when Chie completed a sentence by stealing the punch line to a joke from Fiona, it was the last straw. "Hey!" said Fiona in a half-joking tone, "Speak for yourself!"

Unfortunately, when the American-Japanese interaction is between adversaries or competitors, as it often is in business and in trade, communicators do not give each other the benefit of the doubt as did Chie and Fiona as friends. Instead, cross-cultural communicators who do not understand each other's strategies often come to negative conclusions about the communicators themselves. For example, Americans think of Japanese communicators as "circuitous" and "roundabout," comments Douglas Maynard also makes about the users of perspective display in medical consultations. Neither Listener Talk nor perspective display are the main mode of communication for Americans, so they evaluate them negatively. Similarly, the Japanese often conclude that American communicators are inattentive and selfish. The upfront style in which a speaker speaks her mind in Speaker Talk is not a key criterion of communication for the Japanese, so they evaluate the quality as a liability. In adversarial situations, different communication strategies end up being the proof for previously held misconceptions.

Americans blame the Japanese speaker for being unable to articulate his point of view, and the Japanese blame their American audience for being unable to interpret what the speaker meant.

"How can you be so vague?" ask those in Speaker Talk.

Answer back those in Listener Talk: "But you weren't listening!"

As Americans and Japanese each play their own game, both use strategies that bring out the strength of their own equipment to enhance their play towards their respective goals. Paradoxically, these are also the very strategies that don't make sense to the other side; they are the strategies that compound the initial misunderstanding that has already taken place. Because a general grasp of differences in strategic gameplans can go a long way in reducing the frustration that so often accompanies cross-cultural miscommunication, here are some replays of standard strategies in Speaker Talk and Listener Talk.

Call Me Dave

Just after college, I worked for a Japanese company that had several American subcontractors. My boss, Kawashima, had many dealings with them, but he hardly spoke any English, and was constantly amusing us with examples of his gaffes. There was one that none of us will ever forget.

Kawashima had just come out of his fourth or fifth meeting with the president of one of the company's subcontracted firms. When the President, Dave Williams, finally left, Kawashima, hunched over his desk, began laughing hysterically. This was the section's cue to hear the latest, so we gathered around his desk in anticipation.

"He said, 'Call me Dave,'" said Kawashima, his words choked in laughter. Pronouncing Dave's name with a Japanese accent, Kawashima turned it into *Debu*—a word in Japanese roughly synonymous with fatso in English. Drawing out the "e"-sound in *Debu* makes it a sneer sing-song: "Dave is a fatso!"

Kawashima said he couldn't go on calling Dave "Fatso," and that from the next meeting on, he was going back to "Mr. Williams."

Although enhanced by the "funny" story about mispronouncing Dave's name, the awkwardness in the interaction was really more about a fundamental difference in American and Japanese naming practices. Dave Williams was simply playing a standard strategy in American naming that says, at the appropriate time, choose a name, and say it. Every speaker has the right to choose the time to say how and what he or she wants to be called, and they have the obligation as an individual to communicate that to others. Choosing a name and asking to be called by it is classic Speaker Talk: a spoken piece of independence driven by the speaker.

But for Kawashima, the American strategy seemed odd for several reasons. For starters, the Japanese only call each other by first name if they are intimate members of the same group (uchi). Members of outside groups (soto) otherwise call each other by their last names, plus the word *san,* which is roughly the equivalent of Mr., Mrs., or Ms. except that it does not distinguish between genders. From Kawashima's point of view then, he and Dave Williams are members of different groups; with a soto relationship, the expected Japanese strategy for naming would be, "Williams-san" which translates as, "Mr. Williams."

A second reason Kawashima felt awkward about Dave Williams's strategy of Choose-and-Say naming was because, as he said later, "Japanese don't suddenly declare how they want to be called." Instead, the Japanese "grow into" more intimate ways of calling each other, with women typically moving towards the use of first name plus san, and men, towards the use of last names only without the san-ending. But the drift towards more intimate forms of naming takes much longer, if it happens at all. What's more, even if the changeover had taken place, Kawashima would have called Dave Williams, "Williams" not "Dave."

As the Japanese and Americans struggle to find a mutual system of address, a new trend seems to have developed in recent years, with the Japanese referring to their American colleagues by their first name plus san in a Japanese context, and by their first name alone in an American context. The trend for American names for the Japanese seem to be last name plus san in a Japanese context and first name alone in an American context. With the exception of Japanese references of Americans in an American context, all other situations assume that Choose-and-Say has already occurred. Combining American and Japanese conventions, these cross-cultural strategies seem to have struck a happy middle ground.

Unfortunately, this was not the case with Kawashima and Dave Williams. As it happened, I was present at the next meeting, and though it was not recorded, I vividly remember the conversation that took place. At one point, Kawashima referred to Dave as "Mr. Williams" as he had said he would, and Dave stopped to correct him, saying, "Remember, we're first-name basis now," reminding Kawashima that he had "given permission."

But Kawashima, for the reasons cited, insisted on calling Dave, "Mr. Williams." And Dave, presumably confused, eventually asked, "Would you rather have me call you 'Mr. Kawashima' then?" to which Kawashima responded:

"No, no, no. You call me 'Ryu.' I call you 'Mr. Williams.'"

An awkward focus on the business-at-hand followed. It was a misunderstanding of the worst order because Kawashima's intended respect, "I respect you too much to call you by your first name," turned out to have the reverse effect, "We're not familiar enough to call each other by first name." In trying to call Dave into his field of respectful interdependence, Kawashima ended up looking like a snob.

And that wasn't even the end of it. In a conversation I had later with Dave Williams's assistant, she referred to my boss as "Mr. Kawashima," stressing his title, "*Mister.*" Although Kawashima was anything but the pompous character the assistant was suggesting, it was too late to discredit the insinuation. My boss has been living to regret his choice of naming ever since.

Depends on Who

Once when leaving a university where I was teaching, an American upperclass undergraduate student of Japanese came up to me, and asked with great affection, "So should I call you '*Haru-chan*' now instead of 'Yamada Sensei?'" Chan is a diminutive ending used between friends who have known each other for a long time, usually since childhood, while sensei replaces the san-ending (corresponding roughly with Mr., Mrs. or Ms.) and means "teacher." Yamada Sensei is, then, the equivalent of "Professor Yamada," while Haru-chan glosses as something like "Little Haru."

Since I had a friendly relationship with the student, and since I was no longer formally his professor, from the student's point of view, calling me "Haru-chan" was a legitimate move towards an amicable relationship that was not hierarchical. Remembering graduate students who called a professor by his nickname, I decided the student's suggestion was not as outrageous as it first seemed. Still I couldn't help feeling embarrassed at the sudden intimacy implied in the naming, as well as expelled from my role as the student's professor. His question, intended as warmhearted comraderie, instead made me feel like a child being run out of the university.

So what would a Japanese student have done in the American student's place? First, he would not have asked me what I wanted to be called since, "What should I call you?" is a kind of corollary to the American strategy of Choose-and-Say Naming, "Call me X." Second, a Japanese student would also probably have varied the way he addressed me depending on the context. That is, in the uchi (inside) context of other university members, he may have continued to call me "Yamada Sensei" (Professor Yamada) or just "Sensei" (Professor), while in the soto or outside the university context he may have called me "Yamada-san." Because the relationship still remains hierarchical, a former Japanese student would most probably not call me "Haru-San," even if, say, he became a colleague of mine.

Naming in Japanese is a listener-driven strategy which makes it *depend on who* is present at an interaction. Because people come and go, there is always the potential for group reorganization, and so, a possibility for renaming. This gets confusing even for the Japanese, as illustrated in the "reminders" served up in orientation sessions for entry-level employees. In these sessions, employees are instructed on proper behavior, including how to talk.

Incorporating correct verb forms like those discussed in chapter 2, the sessions use specific examples to demonstrate professionally appropriate speech. When speaking to your boss, for example, use speech that reflects uneven footing: Talk up to him using respectful speech, and humble yourself using humble verb forms. On the telephone, every caller is potentially a client, so always use appropriate speech.[3] Again, talk up to the caller, and humble yourself.

But now imagine you get a call from a client who asks about your boss. The group is now redefined. Both you and your boss together form a unit that uses respectful speech to talk up to the outside (soto) client, and humble speech for the inside (uchi) group. In naming your boss in this instance of Listener Talk, you now treat him like yourself—as humble, stripping his name of the title san (roughly equivalent to Mr., Mrs. or Ms.) and using humble verb forms when talking about him. This is what I did earlier in referring to my boss, Kawashima, without the san-ending. Instead of calling him, "Kawashima-san" (Mr. Kawashima) and raising him above you as readers, I referred to him as I would myself in humble form. Later, when I become more intimate with you, I might refer to others with a san-ending, implying then that we are members of the same (uchi) group, discussing a soto (outside) person in a story.

A similar system of grouping and regrouping also occurs in sports. For example, two American tennis players can play singles against each other in a grand slam tournament, or doubles together against another American doubles pair. But in the Davis Cup or in exhibition matches in the Olympics, all four players can be regrouped to represent the United States.

But like the tennis players involved in regrouping, the Japanese system of Depends-On-Who grouping is not without hiccups even among the Japanese. For one thing, many entry-level employees are uncomfortable about "humbling" their boss in front of their clients—as I often was with my boss sitting right next to me. Fortunately, some useful standard expressions can help you get around sounding like you are stomping on your boss's face. For example, a frequently used formula to say your boss is away from his desk is: [Apologies] + [Last Name of Boss] wa seki o hazushite orimasu ga . . . ([Last Name of Boss] has left his seat).

Still, I have an American friend who, although fluent in Japanese, felt so terrible about "putting his boss down," that he bungled his first attempt to try to say his boss, Tanabe, was away from his desk. In confusing some of the words in, "Tanabe wa seki o hazushite orimasu ga . . . ," he ended up saying, "Tanabe no seki ga hazurete orimasu ga . . . ," which means, "Tanabe's seat is detached"! Suffice it to say that Depends-On-Who naming is tricky business, and if expressions are going to be the order of the day, they have to be learned word for word.

Just Say Yes

A common question asked about the Japanese is why they can't or don't say "no." But this is like asking a soccer player why they don't pick up the ball and run down the field. In each case, the inquirer thinks his way is faster, more efficient, "better." But he is a player from a different game.

In Speaker Talk, "no" is an explicit statement of the individual; it carves out an independent position relative to another. It is ideally unconditional. That is why the "Just Say No" Campaign was mounted as an outright rejection of drugs. Saying "no" meant "no under any circumstance"; it was seen as the way an individual could defend himself, by actively refusing pushy drug dealers.

As the campaign waned, T-shirts and bumper stickers teased back: Just Say Yes. But in practice this would be much more difficult. A "yes" in Speaker Talk is conditional on a number of criteria, and blindly saying "yes" is fatalistic and without careful study. For example, in the following excerpt from a conversation in an American bank meeting, Sandra takes on the job of calling Peter only after she finds out how the other jobs have been distributed.

ANNA: Will you get in touch with Peter?
SANDRA: Is John doing Dunlop?
ANNA: Yeah.
SANDRA: Who's doing ⌈Wilson?
ANNA: ⌊Ja⌈y.
SANDRA: →   ⌊I'll call Peter.

Like the "no" in Listener Talk, the "yes" in Speaker Talk has its shades. Sandra's "yes" is conditional as she accepts getting in touch with Peter only after she confirms that John is taking care of the Dunlop account, and Jay is covering Wilson. "Yes" is conditional to everyone else doing their job because *Yes* + Conditions = guarding the individual. By checking her conditions for acceptance, Sandra keeps herself as an individual intact, making sure that she does not get sucked in and swamped with all the work.

While "yes" can threaten independence in Speaker Talk, "yes" in Listener Talk is desirable because it reinforces the interdependent message, "Yes, I'm with you." Emphasizing this message of interdependence means that the message of individual agreement found in Speaker Talk that says, "Yes, I agree with you," or "Yes, I will carry out action X" is secondary. This does not mean that the Japanese never mean "yes"—there are ways of saying, "definitely 'yes'" like, "kanarazu itashimasu" (I will definitely do it). But what it does mean is that in places where interdependence and smooth relations are necessary, such as in business, negative points will be softened as much as possible so that the overall image is one of "yes."

Unfortunately, this Japanese strategy is the cause of great confusion for players of Speaker Talk who often end up thinking the Japanese don't mean it when they say "yes." Said President Clinton: "When the Japanese say 'yes' they mean 'no.'" Not fully understanding the strategic use and purpose of the Japanese "yes," players in Speaker Talk can only conclude that "yes" means the opposite of what it means to them.

The way the Japanese use "no" is also different but not opposite from the American variety. There are more than a dozen different ways of saying "no" without actually using the word "iie" (no), and these standard expressions are considered to be softer and therefore better for maintaining interdependence. An example of a softened "no" appeared in an exchange cited earlier where a Japanese bank executive, Maeda, totally disagreed with his colleague, Igarashi, about a proposal. Asked to comment on it, Maeda said, "Sore wa chotto . . . ," which literally means, "That's a little . . . ," instead of saying, "No, I disagree with it entirely," or, "Definitely not": "Zettai dame desu." Foregoing a categorical disagreement which would emphasize his contradictory opinion and possibly jeopardize his rapport with Igarashi, Maeda opted for a softer way of saying, "no."

Once many summers ago, the soft "no" came in handy when I was waitressing at a Japanese restaurant where the owner asked me out on a date. Although I was not interested, I couldn't just say "no"—the owner was my boss and I needed the job. So I said, "Let me think about it," which is a standard way of saying, "Probably not." Had the owner come back and asked me for an answer a few days later I would have been in trouble. But like other Japanese, he had understood that the answer was probably going to be "no" even a few days later. Unless he really didn't care about embarrassing himself, "Let me think about it" was enough of a hint for him to interpret a "no." When I later told my mother about the interaction, she chuckled saying, "You said that?" implying I was being slightly audacious. Although "Let me think about it" may not sound at all like a "no" to non-Japanese, for the Japanese, it is plenty unequivocal, even to the point of sounding overly forward.

While lines like "I'll think about it" also occur in American dating relationships where interdependent feelings are a delicate and primary matter, Americans would not expect to hear them in formal settings where explicit communication is seen as tantamount. But because the Japanese do—their interdependent relationships stretch across private and public spheres—there is an enormous potential for misunderstanding as a softened "no" aimed at minimizing the threat to interdependent relationships ends up being mistaken for "yes." This was presumably what happened in the now famous incident between former Prime Minister Sato and ex-President Nixon. As Prime Minister Sato said, "Zensho shimasu," ([I'll] try [my] best/hardest) in regard to changing the practice of Japanese textile exports to the U.S., President Nixon took it to mean, "yes," and was later disappointed to find that nothing had changed. Although "Zensho shimasu," ([I'll] try [my] best/hardest) does not mean "definitely not," it is usually used as a negative warning. It is a way of saying, "I'll try my hardest, but it probably won't work out," as opposed to the American expectation that it probably will work out. Different strategic uses of "yes" and "no" result in different interpretations of what "thinking about it" or "trying your hardest" means for Americans and for Japanese. The rule of thumb for players of Speaker Talk is then to actively monitor the shades of Japanese "yes" and "no," and not to conclude that they always mean the opposite of what they would mean in English.

In short, that the Japanese do not often say the word "no" then, does not mean they never refuse anything or turn things down. There are ways in Listener Talk for saying, "I don't agree with that," "I don't want to do that," or "Let's not talk about that." But they are presented in a way that prioritizes interdependent relationship. "Yes" and "no" are not exactly equivalent in Japanese and in English, and understanding a word in another communicative game is not as simple as looking a word up in an English-Japanese dictionary. That is why asking a

Japanese why they never actually say the word "no" makes as little sense as mounting a Just Say Yes Campaign.

Have a Nice Day

There was a time when English subtitles for Japanese films were painfully literal. Lines like, "Oh honorable Father sir, I beg you to look kindly upon me," littered screens, from gritty black and white to modern color. To get "honorable Father sir," the subtitler had dissected the word for father, *otoosan,* into its components: Honorable *o* + "father" *too* + "Mr." or "sir" *san.*

For the Japanese, calling your father otoosan is the equivalent of calling your father "Dad" in English. Like our grandfather who we may not think of as a particularly "grand" version of our father, we call him "Grandfather" despite the fact that it has lost its original and literal meaning. Much of Japanese is confused in this way through literal translation and interpretation into English, and there is no better example of this than the stereotype of the polite Japanese.

An example that is often used to poke fun at the so-called "polite" nature of the Japanese is the phrase, "*doozo, doozo*" (after you, after you). One well-known joke is about a pregnant woman who visits her obstetrician because she is worried about being past her due date. When the doctor listens in with his stethoscope, there are two voices—twins—each going, "Doozo, doozo" (after you, after you), "Doozo, doozo" (after you, after you). Anyone who has been to Japan has also probably witnessed the countless number of elevators held in suspension while Japanese communicators play out their standoff match of "doozo, doozo." But while conventional expressions like "doozo, doozo" alleviate players from having to gamble their relationships on untested talk, giving communicators a chance to practice a standard play in the Japanese field of interdependence, I have had enoughs jabs and seat-swiping in the subway to know that the Japanese are no more polite than the next guy.

The Japanese have the reputation of being polite because their need for interdependence creates dozens of standard expressions in thanking, apologizing and inviting others to go first, which when translated literally, sound comically polite. But for the Japanese who use them, they are remarkably ordinary, sometimes even to the point of emptiness. Like the Americans with "Have a nice day," the Japanese use standard expressions to smooth out the links of everyday relationships without necessarily literally meaning every word they say.

I mention "Have a nice day" because this American expression once snowballed into a debate in a class I was teaching in London. We were talking about metaphor—how words, phrases and sentences can take on meanings other than their literal ones. "Have a nice day," I said, was a commercial way of saying, "Thank you": "Thanks for shopping with us," or "Thanks for using our service."

But this provoked a reaction in the class. "This is precisely why Americans are so false," said an English student. "They say things like that with this big fake smile on their face, and they don't really mean it."

"But you do the same thing," said a Polish student. "The English say, 'sorry' all the time and they don't really mean it. It's just their way of sweeping bad things under the rug. They think if they're sorry, everything will be all right. They'll be forgiven and it'll all go away."

The discussion among the students highlighted a fundamental misperception about language that meaning is—and *should be*—literal. But the linguist George Lakoff and the philosopher Mark Johnson point out that exactly the reverse is true: Metaphor is not a mere poetic embellishment to what we think of as our "regular language"; we use and interpret metaphor in our everyday language.[4] For example, when speakers of English, using the metaphor "Argument is War," say, "He attacked every weak point in my argument," "Your claims are indefensible," or "I demolished his argument," we know what the metaphors mean and not to interpret them literally.

But as the English and Polish students demonstrated in turn, a metaphor is interpreted literally if the concept is absent in your own communicative field. For the English student, commercialism and salesmanship are not as prevalent in the United Kingdom as they are in the United States. Consequently, the student interprets "Have a nice day" as insincere because she doesn't see the friendliness intended by the message. She has no context in which to interpret the metaphor, so she interprets it literally. Similarly, apologies are only offered in grave circumstances in Poland so the Polish student doesn't see why the English apologize for lesser offenses. She interprets apologies in such situations as false in literal terms because that kind of apologizing is unknown to her.

The same thing happens when Americans hear conventional expressions of thanks and apologies by the Japanese, and interpret them as great or excessive politeness. Because Americans interact with a focus on independence, they misinterpret the Japanese need for interdependence as going to great lengths to "be nice to each other." But for the players of Listener Talk, they are just making standard gestures to show that they are playing the game of interdependence through implicit communication. What seems excessive then, whether they are Americans judging Japanese, British judging Americans, or Polish judging British, is whatever does not occur in their own communicative field—whatever they are not used to.

Misunderstandings also occur when blame is assigned to others because the kind of communication you are used to does not occur. When Americans go into British stores where salespeople do not participate in "Have a nice day" salesmanship, they often judge the British as having no sense of customer service. Similarly, when the Japanese interact with Americans and an apology or a thanks—albeit a formality—does not occur where they expect it to, the Japanese think of Americans as gruff or ungrateful.

A final note on politeness is that while the Japanese are not always being polite when they are using polite expressions, that does not mean that the Japanese are phony all the time, but only that their drive to be connected is so strong that appearances are kept up at potential cost to sincerity. Japanese expect this discrepancy, naming the emphasis on appearance *tatemae* (principle), and contrasting it with the holding back of true feelings of honne through *enryo* (reservation). Only careful listenership can weed out the true from the feigned, the sincere from the front.

If you ask the Japanese how they can tell the difference, they will tell you, "we just know." This is not as unhelpful a pointer as it first seems. Americans "just know" too whether someone signing off a letter, "Love, so-and-so" means they're really thinking a lot about you, or whether they really mean, "Have a nice day."

Greetings of Action, Greetings of Care

A Japanese friend, Kawase, recently told me about how American greetings made him anxious. "They say things like, 'How're you doing?' 'What's happening?' and 'What's up?' and I always feel like I have to say something interesting about what I have been doing. Unfortunately, I'm just a salaryman [business person], and my life is pretty boring."

Here is another case of a literal interpretation of expressions that are intended as metaphorical: When Americans ask each other "What's happening?" they don't really mean for you to give them a complete summary of what has happened to you since you last saw them. Unless you are good friends and have the time to sit down and chat, a greeting like, "What's up?" is treated as a conventional expression like "How are you?"

Japanese greetings are also metaphorical—just as with Americans, no one expects you to give you a rundown on how you actually are. But American and Japanese greetings are different in two ways. First, the Japanese favor conventional responses to greetings, while Americans prefer ones that are more individualized. This does not mean that American responses are altogether original, but that a variation from, "Fine thank you, and you?" is considered more interesting, and more hip—in short, preferable. The Japanese on the other hand can use alternative greetings and responses but their expectation is for the conventional.

Second, Americans and Japanese evoke different metaphors in their greetings: Many American greetings conjure up a metaphor of action, while Japanese ones call up an image of care. "How're you doing," "What's up," "How's it going," "What's happening," all show that for Americans, how you are is defined by activity; how you are is what you are doing. But salutations like, "taihen gobusata shite orimasu" (roughly, "please excuse me for not calling sooner") and "itsumo osewa sama de gozaimasu" (roughly, "thanks for always taking care of me"), "doozo yoroshiku onegai itashimasu" (roughly, "please look after me," used similarly as the English "nice to meet you"), and responses like "okagesama de," (roughly, "because of you, I'm feeling well") all show that for the Japanese, well-being is defined in terms of interdependent care.

A Japanese like Kawase feels uncomfortable with American greetings, then, because the Japanese don't ask questions of well-being based on action. Instead, they ask—and expect in return—metaphors of connection and care. The unease is replicated in the other direction too, as Americans often feel embarrassed when the Japanese respond with, "I'm well because of you." Because Americans do no greet each other with the metaphor of care, such expressions are taken literally. An American tax consultant, John, once told me he responded to "Thanks for always looking after me," with, "You're welcome," where a Japanese might have answered, "No, it's you who has been looking after me," practicing the Others-Centered philosophy and interacting with the metaphor of care. Because Americans and Japanese call up different metaphors in their initial contact, both sides feel uncomfortable when they are asked to play in a communicative field where the images of relationship are different.

In some ways, the difference between Speaker Talk and Listener Talk is all about the different metaphors of action and care. When an American speaker chooses the moment for saying how he wants to be called by others, he is *acting* upon his right in the field of independence to do so. Similarly, a Japanese listener keeps tabs on the communicators to know how to address them in a way that reflects their care and togetherness.

For "yes" and "no" strategies too, American speakers see themselves as taking action on their individual positions that are juxtaposed against others, while Japanese listeners view themselves as saying, "yes" or "no" to enhance the dynamics of group care. Finally, conventional expressions like, "Have a nice day" evoke an image of an American salesperson taking an active role in how you spend your future, while "Maido arigatoo gozaimasu" (roughly, "thanks for shopping with us all the time") summons an image of a Japanese salesperson thanking you for a continual store/shopper relationship of care.

Americans and Japanese use different strategies in naming, saying "yes" or "no," and in using conventional expressions. Such differences arise because Americans define the ideal communicator as a speaker-in-action, while the Japanese define the ideal communicator as a listener who cares. In cross-cultural interaction, simple misunderstandings are complicated by mutual misinterpretations of each other's strategies, and the guiding motive in each player's gameplan. Because a better understanding of different gameplans can only be gained by comparing specific American and Japanese communicative strategies, the following five chapters examine business and present some playouts in the sport of business communication.

Basic Strategies For Players of Speaker Talk

- Always add -san to the names of others, but never your own. Refer to yourself by just your last name, and identify yourself with the name of your organization.
- Try to assess your role in the communication. How do you fit in? Closely monitor your role as it can change from setting to setting.
- Take extra precaution when interpreting "yes" and "no." If the encounter is important enough, get a native speaker to interpret alongside yours. Study carefully what you understand as "yes" in particular—it might be a shaded "no."
- If you use standard expressions, make sure you learn them word for word, and know how to use them. Don't just look them up in a dictionary and expect to use them appropriately.
- Remember to use as many expressions of care as possible.

Basic Strategies For Players of Listener Talk

- Let each person decide for him or herself how they want to be addressed. Then, address them in the way that they ask.
- Try not to use a shaded "no." It is often confusing for players unfamiliar with Listener Talk.
- Don't be put off by what seems like a lack of thanks, apology or care. Use as many expressions of action as possible instead.

4

Taking Care of Business

Some people believe that the primary job of business managers is to deal with numbers. But as the sociologist Mintzberg notes, "verbal contacts, face-to-face and on the phone, account for 75% of a managers' time, and 67% of their activities."[1] Business is as much communication as it is quantification because at the end of the day, numbers are defended, negotiated, and sold; they are interpreted and *communicated*. American and Japanese business and business communication is, then, really an example of the larger society in which it takes place.

Because business communication takes place in a particular language such as English or Japanese, in this chapter, I argue against the popular notion of a universal "Business Culture" that floats above nations. Instead, I demonstrate how American and Japanese business are each subject to their own criteria for evaluation. The boundaries of communication and relationship that define American and Japanese interaction in general also define interaction in business.[2]

Business is Business, Business is Family

My first job after college was in market research for a Japanese real estate developer in the United States. My main duties were to perform feasibility studies, administrate bids, and liaise with the personnel responsible for contracts in the various counties. But after a few months of work, I was asked to participate in sales, which increasingly meant late nights and weekends. One day, I complained about this to a friend, Louise, and she responded: "Why don't you just tell them that sales isn't part of your job—that it's not in your job description."

I was surprised that Louise had reframed my predicament as one I could actually do something about. But I was even more surprised by the suggestion of correcting my boss by pointing to a job description that circumscribed the boundaries of my work. Looking at my job from the American perspective then, I began to see that it was within my legal rights to ensure that my employers kept to their contract. After all, said Louise, employers don't want to abuse their employees. It's bad business. And, standing up to them would only send them a message they expect—that I was willing to do my job—no more or no less. I was enough of a person to protect my own rights, so they should be the kind of employer who kept to their word.

When I finally did get around to asking the director of personnel for a job description, she began leafing through the files of her cabinet without hesitation. Halfway through, however, she turned around and said, "Oh, I forgot. Japanese employees don't have job descriptions, it's only for the American employees."

By marking off the boundaries of a player's work, a job description is business shorthand for the American expectation of independence. But the Japanese operate with a different unwritten rule: Instead of individual rights that segregate and define a person's position, their preference is for the overlap of interdependent positions. In such a system, a member of a group does whatever task is appropriate to their rank. Like a ball boy who also gets a player drinks or towels in addition to his main job of picking up tennis balls off the courts, lower ranking members of a company like me, play the role of gophers. Similarly, like the tennis player who serves, volleys, and hits ground strokes, managerial tasks for executives also remain eclectic and general. The role of Japanese managers and executives differs from those of their colleagues in American companies where jobs become more specialized the higher the rank; for these players, their game is more like American football where each player's job is task-specific. If Japanese companies were to institute a system of job descriptions, then, they would have to be ones that cover the range of tasks that occur at every rank level, and not a system of job descriptions like the American one that lists the tasks required of individual positions.

Interdependence defines the relationships of Japanese business players. Beginning at the larger organizational level, Japanese business closely resembles a family tree where a network of companies in oya-ko kankei (parent-child relations) presents each bun or part as a ko (child) in relation to an oya (parent), another bun (part). Vertical networks connect ko-gaisha child companies to the parent oya-gaisha company, and lateral networks connect cousin subsidiaries to a grandparent company. Internally, densely nested networks of amae (sweetness) interdependence connect those in the uchi (inside), so that, like Russian dolls, the company contains the family, which contains individuals. In the context of uchi-soto kankei, or inside-outside relationships, amae encircles those in the uchi (inside), while it excludes those in the soto (outside). This nested construction of interdependence is reflected in an employee's self-introduction: Said first is the company name as the largest organizer, followed by the family name, and finally and optionally, the bun or fractional part, the first name.

The superficial structure of a Japanese company may seem no different from an American one. The difference is in the effect of the structure on internal relationships: Japanese employees really act as if they are family members who count on each other and the organization to take part in or organize various aspects of their personal lives. This is in part why Japanese business relationships extend far beyond the regular workday—late-night drinking and rounds of golf are seen as part of work—as they are a part of everyday life. It also helps explain why Japanese companies don't have job descriptions. Just as your role in the family is implicit and unwritten, so too is your role at work: Business is family.

Also demonstrating the blurred distinction between the characteristics that define business and family in Japan, it is not uncommon for a company to make funeral arrangements for an employee, supplying anything from financial sponsorship to company helpers who aid in the ceremony. Unless the deceased is a high-ranking public figure, a company funeral for Americans would be an inappropriate crossover into private life. Compared to the Japanese, American relationships are more strictly divided between the personal, made up of friends and family, and business. Although some business colleagues might become friends, and relatives might work in the same company, most American business players believe that work and play are best kept separate. As the old saying suggests, "Don't mix business with pleasure." Business is business.

Simply understanding how the principle of familial interdependence operates could facilitate remembering the dos and don'ts of how to exchange meishi (business cards), the now famous "must-know" among Japanese business survival tips. Treat the *meishi* you receive as you would your best friend's grandmother: You wouldn't put a meishi in your back pocket, just as you wouldn't sit on your best friend's grandmother.

Customized versus Shared Work

In chapter 1, I discussed how the American ideal for independence makes its mark on space. In business, there is the psychological space of a job title and description discussed earlier, but there is also a physical space at work: a desk, a phone, a PC. The more prestigious the job, the more of these "customized" gadgets you have. The portable phone is the ultimate symbol of independence. It shows that you can control your own time and communication—no one else tells you what to do.

Independence is also about the ownership of power because taking care of an individual piece of business—an account, a case, or a project means you exercise control over it. Take, for example, shares in a business: The bigger your share, the more you own it, and the more you control it. If you have the biggest share, or if you monopolize the shares, you have the most control—you are the most independent.

Another kind of independent ownership has to do with the degree to which you customize your own job. The more you customize your job, the more autonomous you become because it makes you more indispensable. Take computers: By customizing various features in programs, they simultaneously become more "yours" and more difficult for others to use. By protecting your own property, customization serves as an application of the American ideal of independence.

Given this evidence of customization, in a perfect American world, everyone would have their own business. But the dynamics of commercial competition (otherwise known as capitalism) exclude this as a possibility because while free competition is not in itself a problem, it does have the potential to create inequalities in the distribution of wealth. Because American history depicts a past in which settlers fled the gross inequalities of wealth in Europe to found a country in which equality was upheld as an ideal, written into the American consciousness is the influential and unifying belief that equality should be sought whenever possible. Says the psychologist Roman Barboa: "We all have equal worth, equal value."[3]

Because the American ideal of equality clashes with independence, modern American institutions often incorporate a regulated method of conditional independence which I have been calling Equal Opportunity Independence. Rules are set so that the strongest are also the most heavily taxed; they have a handicap to level the playing field. The weaker, in contrast, are aided. From affirmative action to managed international trade, Equal Opportunity Independence is basic to American business as it maximizes the advantages of individual competition, while minimizing potential monopolies.

On an everyday basis, Equal Opportunity Independence shows up in written agendas that dictate reporting rounds in meetings. For example, in an American bank meeting I studied, each of the three participants comes forth and reports on their *own* business according to the agenda. As each person reports on his or her own customized business, they each credit themselves as individuals. At the same time, a set agenda gives everyone a chance to do this, so in the end, each and everyone can achieve both equality and independence.

In contrast to customization, the Japanese workplace fosters familial interdependence. Instead of dividing office space into individually bounded rooms or cubicles, for example, it is left open, in a bullpen. Another example of familial interdependence is the Japanese manager's role in creating an environment in which employees perceive themselves as working together for a common goal. In section meetings, the manager draws the focus away from internally competitive and individualized aspects of the job, and refocuses the group on shared ventures, such as program planning, scheduling, and comments on proposals in circulation. Throughout the fiscal year, the manager also shares projects or accounts across members of his section. As the entire section shares in a day's work, open spaces are seen as ideal for facilitating informal meetings called *uchiawase,* where a boss calls upon subordinates to chat about a variety of eclectic topics.

The "sound-outs" on views and positions that take place in these short and frequent uchiawase meetings provide a major resource for the Japanese process of consensus decision building called *nemawashi* (literally, root-binding). Together with other conversations that occur among workmates at every level throughout the work day, and in bars, restaurants, golf courses and other venues of entertainment, managers use uchiawase to sound out the feasibility of proposals that are currently circulating through the company.

The rationale for such background consensus building is the Japanese belief that the more intimate the relationship, the greater the chance for the expression of true feelings on a given proposal. A good sampling of true feelings is more likely to lead to a better decision on advancing or dropping a proposal, and a proposal that everyone endorses is more likely to succeed. In such a system of nemawashi (consensus decision building), which builds a proposition with the greatest likelihood for support, by the time the time-consuming process culminates in a written proposal that is passed around the company for approval, and presented in a formal meeting for final approbation, the decision is usually already made. Unlike the equality in American business, which is distributed in projects and negotiated in meetings through a written agenda, equality in Japanese business is attained by giving everyone a chance to contribute their opinions and decisions through the *uchiawase* meetings.

The different locuses of decision gathering and building, and the resulting differences in the way American and Japanese meetings are carried out, lead to widespread misunderstanding. Americans often voice frustration when they come out of Japanese meetings that seem stiff and staged. Such impressions are created by pro-forma meetings where the outcome is already known when Americans are expecting a decision-oriented negotiation.

First-timers in Japan often only get to see these "fait accompli" performances where a meeting is held post-facto because, in the early phases of a business relationship, there is little or no expectation of amae (sweetness) interdependence, the basis of uchiawase (sound-out) meetings. But without knowing this, and without knowing that even an initial meeting is a positive outcome of a decision to move forward already made through consensus nemawashi (decision building), it is easy to jump to the conclusion that all Japanese meetings are stiff and ceremonial, or worse, that the Japanese themselves are cold and robotic. "At least they look that way in meetings," said one executive after returning from his first trip to Japan.

Such a misguided first impression is exacerbated by the fact that studies of organizational behavior in the United States give greater coverage to the ceremonious meetings, professionally confirming the Japanese reputation of being "formal." Important formalities must be learned in order to do business with the Japanese, goes this school of thought. But this reasoning barks up the wrong tree.

The formal and ritual meetings are highly structured, and so, more comprehensible than uchiawase (sound-outs). But for Americans, these meetings are also the initial ones, and in them, there is little that can be "done" in the way of getting a decision. At this stage, the Japanese are checking out the American company and its members, and they are less interested in the specific details of a prod-

uct or service than in finding out whether they want to pursue a business relationship at all. In these early meetings, then, a positive and appealing self-pre-
sentation is more likely to reap productive results than an intensified sales pitch.
This can be accomplished by understanding in-house uchiawase meetings—ones
that successful American business people eventually get to know, but ones that
are least studied or understood.

Unfortunately, because of the misperception that the formal meetings are the
real and important ones, Americans who eventually take part in uchiawase
(sound-out) meetings often end up dismissing them as illogical and unbusi-
nesslike; these formally less structured meetings without written agendas seem
pointless and unwieldy. Also surprising to many Americans is the intimate, non-
business tone of these Japanese meetings because for Americans, part of what
makes business business, and distinguishable from pleasure is the absence of "personal" feelings. It is the kind of protocol that Miss Manners prescribes in "professionalism": "In business, being pleasant and efficient, without exposing one's
private emotions is called professional demeanor."[4]

Here's an example. On *Larry King*, Eric Menendez's lawyer Leslie Abramsen was asked by a caller how she felt about her heated exchange with Judge Jack
Tenner. She responded that she didn't care how much they yelled at each other
because the point of the trial was to get at the truth, not to get "personal." Like
Abramsen, many Americans distinguish between the unemotional quality of
work, and personal feelings that supposedly belong outside the workplace.

But for the Japanese, the circles of work and play overlap to a greater degree,
accounting in part for why Japanese meetings are built on intimate sound-outs
with a substantial proportion taken up in what the organizational behaviorists
Graham and Sano call "nontask sounding" talk: Conversation that sounds like
chit-chat to Americans, but essential conversation to the Japanese who view the
more personal conversation as an opportunity to reaffirm amae (sweetness) ties
with members of the company. In general, the higher the level of the meeting,
the more intimate the relationship of communicators and consequently the more
nontask sounding talk there is.

I once recorded a personnel bank meeting between a Japanese executive vice
president, Takagi, and an American senior vice President, Jane, in which nontask
sounding took up about one third of the meeting time. Albeit company related,
Takagi talked about upcoming entertainment, dinner, theater, and so on, until
they finally got down to discussing the "real business" of various new personnel
assignments twenty minutes later. Jane, a veteran in dealing with Japanese executives, said later that she understood the irritation some Americans felt during
such long sound-outs. Especially when the relationship is external and competitive rather than internal and cooperative, Americans are likely to interpret the
nontask sounding talk as a crude tactic in stalling.

On the other hand, from the Japanese end, thrashing out ideas and decisions
in an American meeting seems like a hopeless showcase of selfish desires, each

person yelling out in turn what they want. Such confrontation appears chaotic and detrimental to the health of relationships in the long-term because even in business, physical and psychological space is shared among Japanese business players in the unwritten interdependence of Listener Talk, but customized among American business players who seek to achieve Equal Opportunity Independence in Speaker Talk.

Individual Choice, Group Ensemble

Despite my repeated Pacific crossings and familiarity with American ways, I always seem to have a communication crisis when I reach the front of the line in a deli. The moment of truth comes when I try to accomplish what I think is the simple task of ordering a sandwich.

> White, whole wheat, rye or pumpernickel?
> Whole wheat, I say with decisiveness.
> But there's more: Lettuce, tomato, onions and mayo?
> Anything on the side? Fries, coleslaw a pickle?
> Anything to drink? Coke, Diet Coke or Pepsi?
> Anything else? For here or to go?

Ordering lunch in Japan seems so much easier since ready-made choices are available in a number of ensembles. At a *sobaya* (noodle shop), for example, a number of different kinds of noodle soups with different toppings and different names are available, often with pictures in a menu, or plastic displays in a glass case. An order is placed by name (or by number) from among these ensembles in a way similar to placing an order from among the menu at a McDonald's. Because the choice is of a ready-made ensemble, lunch-goers in Japan typically do not ask for more of one topping than another, an extra, or something on the side. Choice is among ensembles, not within.

For Americans, on the other hand, choice occurs not only among ensembles (pastrami or chicken salad sandwich), but also within (type of bread and potential ingredients of a sandwich). That's why every time I recover from the marathon questioning in a deli line, I remind myself that I am being given the right to exercise my freedom of choice. Like the Burger King motto, "Have it your way," from the contents of a sandwich to a lifestyle, choice is the right of every American resident.

Choice is not only a right, it is also power. Those who can pick and choose are in an advantageous position, but someone who doesn't have a choice is in a weak position. It is someone who can only fatalistically say, "I had to do it. I had no choice."

Because the powerful have a choice, where there is power there is choice—or at least, so the powerful make it seem. Remember the taped instruction on *Mission Impossible:* "Your mission, should you choose to accept it. . . ." Everyone knows that the actors are going to undertake the impossible mission, and that they don't really have a choice. But the message is crafted so that it seems like a mission that only the omnipotent would take on, and therefore, a mission they would choose.

Another example of the message, "choice gives you power" is found in a clever message at the end of a transatlantic flight: "Thank you for flying with X Airlines. When it comes to air carriers, we know you have a choice, and we appreciate your choosing us." By praising its passengers for making the right choice, this soft sales pitch encourages passengers to fly with them again despite other incentives for choosing a particular carrier like low cost for economy travelers and frequent-flyer miles for others.

Choice also sells because it gives people the sense of ownership. When my custom-made sandwich was put together, it was practically monogrammed with my name. It became my own sandwich—mine and no one else's because I made my own choices for its contents. Choice sells because it individualizes power.

This same idea of ownership by individual choice is also found in American Speaker Talk: If you choose to talk or write, you own that talk or writing. What you have said or written is yours because you have committed yourself in air time or on paper. Saying and writing pay tribute to the individual's right to choose and own, and exercising the right—like in the deli—is a kind of everyday parade for independence. While Americans positively evaluate talk that appears customized, they view undifferentiated talk left without the mark of an individual less favorably. Sliding into cliched talk is unexciting, and taking others' individualized writing is what we call plagiarism.

In contrast, in Japanese Listener Talk, set expressions that might be considered cliche among Americans are expected, particularly on ceremonial occasions. The standard expression, *goshuushoosama* (my sympathies for you) at a funeral, for example, is customary. An American friend once told me a story about a funeral she went to for a Japanese friend who died from a ruptured cerebral embolism (a blockage of the blood vessel in the brain). In trying to convey her deepest sympathies in her own words to the deceased's mother, she thought it would be more sympathetic if she said a sentence or two in Japanese. The sentence she wanted to say was that her deceased friend, Kayo was a really fun person to be with. So she said: Kayo wa totemo okashii hito deshita (Kayo was a very funny person).

Although *okashii* can mean "funny" in different ways, okashii hito (funny person) usually means, "funny in the head." Fortunately, because the deceased's family had spent some time in the United States, the sentence produced a moment of comic, if dark, relief. The point here is that the use of the standard expression, goshuushoosama deshita (my sympathies) would have been more appropriately Japanese, and although not as unique, more appreciated.

The Japanese director Ozu made a film called *Sooshiki* (*The Funeral*) that presents another example of the comical side of formalities in funerals. In the course of funeral preparations, the family of the deceased rent an instructional video that demonstrates a long version of a formulaic speech of thanks for condolences, and a short one for those who are too overcome with grief. Everyone opts for the short form.

Unlike American communication where individualized expressions are considered more personal, sincere and creative, the Japanese use standard expressions to promote interdependence. Comfort is found in hearing what is supposed to be heard because, for the Japanese, it is more considerate, sensitive and unassuming. In contrast to plagiarism, then, where copying an individual's words is considered negatively as stealing, the Japanese expect set phrases and texts, and omitting them, like omitting to express feelings "in your own words" for Americans, is a violation.

While this may make it seem as though there is no choice in Japan, a quick look at the quantity of omiyage (souvenirs, like regional food brought to those back home), and the vast number of vending machines at train stations filled with a variety of drinks and other products gives evidence of choice in Japan. But Japanese-style choice differs from the American in kind: While a Japanese chooses among given, pre-packaged choices, an American customizes her own choice. This means that an American strives to obtain a special choice that no one else has, while a Japanese desires the comfort of choosing an accepted variety, one that is not too different from others.

The political scientist Mushakooji Kinhide also differentiates two kinds of choice, calling the western variety *erabi* (choice), and the Japanese one, *awase* (adapting).[5] Mushakooji argues that erabi logic is a best-choice selection from among a set of alternatives in an environment that is assumed to be manipulable, while awase logic works by adapting to an environment that is assumed to be ever-changing. Erabi works best in black and white where rules are clear-cut, while awase works best in the diffuse grey zone. Another way of putting this is that Americans create choice, whereas Japanese select choice through a process of elimination; Americans choose by picking the chosen item, but Japanese derive the chosen item by crossing off other available alternatives.

In Japan Town in San Francisco, I recently saw an example of the difference between erabi (choice) and awase (adapting) logic. A problem emerged with an item at the head of the line in one of the express lanes in the supermarket. When the line came to a standstill, two middle-aged Japanese women who were next in line practiced awase choice by reloading their groceries into a basket and moving over to the next checkout counter, which had a longer line and was non-express. The adaptation of the Japanese woman presented an interesting contrast to the next person in line, an American woman, who, putting her basket on the floor, said to the cashier: "I chose this aisle because it was '*express.*'" Her erabi choice already made, this woman stuck it out in the express aisle.

Another example from business is the standard process of hiring entry-level employees. Japanese companies select their annual slate of new employees from the top universities by taking the top X percentile. Apart from those who have a special "in," this crop of incoming employees receive pro-forma interviews, and the assumption that they are the best candidates for the entry-level positions drives the decision that is already made. If the offer is declined (a scenario that is less common in Japan than in the United States), then personnel hires the next person down on the ranked list. Although the principle of slate selection can be similar in the United States especially in hiring for training programs, no one automatically hires the top percentile from the top universities. Indeed what is considered "top" is much more varied and less prepackaged, and employees are interviewed and hired in a one-by-one selection process that is repeated each time an offer is turned down. Say the education specialists Chambers and Cummings:

> Japan is a more centralized society, whether in government, economy or education. Partly for this reason, Japanese eyes focus on a more restricted set of employers as the most attractive places to work, including the central government and the select group of large firms. These employers tend to concentrate their recruitment efforts at a small number of universities, enhancing the attractiveness of these institutions as places for ambitious young people to study. In the United States, good jobs go to graduates of the more prestigious colleges and universities, but the linkage is not so tight, or at least it is not perceived as being so tight. Americans are not as homogeneous in the perceptions of preferred employers, and the routes to good jobs tend to be more varied: from college yes, but also from graduate school or following experience at the workplace. Because top colleges do not have as clear a monopoly on top jobs, and do not stand so high in the United States, less competitive colleges possibly do not sit so low.[6]

American-style recruiting is in a sense an example of American-style choice-making. Like the airlines announcement cited earlier, recruiters make their companies attractive so that the final decision to choose is perceived as belonging to the recruit. Not so in Japan, where an employee is invited to be a part of a group, and not to make an individual and distinctive contribution like the American employee. For Americans, hiring and working for a company are explicit choices negotiated individually, but for Japanese, mutually adapted choices are assumed between company personnel and university recruits.

A similar process takes place in selecting contractors or business partners. Collecting a number of estimates through *mitsumori,* a Japanese company tries to envision their relationship with the various companies that have submitted proposals for a possible alliance. Compared not only for cost but also for the value of a long-term relationship, the companies who submit their mitsumori (estimates) are often those who are members of a larger and shared consortium (which may be a *zaibatsu,* a large financial clique, like Mitsubishi Corporation).

By contrast, in selecting their best business alliance, American companies do not necessarily rely on an established group of associated firms. Instead, an organization is selected from a larger pool of competitive proposals. What's more, when the term for the relationship expires, the process repeats itself so that unprofitable relationships are terminated and replaced by those that are more competitive.

Japanese companies, on the other hand, are less likely to sever relatively unproductive relationships because of the belief that internal competition weakens and distracts, and is ultimately less cost-effective than relegating unproductive relationships to the back burner. In short, erabi (choice), often formally upheld in a business contract, defines an agreement among individuals to exercise their right to make choices. Awase (adapting), on the other hand, is a tacit agreement among Japanese adapters to match each other in an ensemble. Unlike the American constitution, which clearly identifies the American ideal of the freedom of choice, the concept of awase is absent from the Japanese constitution, and in business, written documentation like a mitsumorisho (written estimate) is often pro-forma.[7] Instead of the negotiation of individual choices, the Japanese depend on each other for mutual adaptation in awase.

In cross-cultural interaction, Americans see a playing field where there is no individual choice making as unfair and rigged. Awase (adapting choice in interdependence) creates the basis for *kashi-kari* interaction among the Japanese, which literally means "lend-borrow," and refers to giving and receiving favors. A favor might be returned to you, for example, by employing your son in the favor-returner's company. Alternatively, you might begin the cycle and "borrow" a favor, and expect to return the favor at a later date. Japanese kashi-kari is not dissimilar to the western concept of "owing someone a favor," but is more formalized to the extent that a favor can be returned in the form of cash. To outsiders, this aspect of kashi-kari is often interpreted as a bribe.

As part of the Japanese decision-making process, kashi-kari (giving and receiving favors) and other reciprocal interactions form a densely interwoven network which makes Japanese society seem exclusive. "The Japanese market is closed," is an oft-cited view among Americans who find group-based decision making impenetrable compared to their "open entry" decision making style, which clears prior debts and examines each contract and business alliance anew on a one-to-one basis. But for the Japanese, the American system that treats each relationship as novel seems time-consuming and undermining of trust. Without the advantage of historical relationships, decisions seem short-term and self-defeating. The question the Japanese ask is: Why would you want to tire yourself out in intramural matches when there are greater competitive matches to face?

Outside familiar territory and without intelligible guidelines for procedures, both sides end up swinging around in the dark. Frustrated Americans sometimes bully their way into Japanese companies, presenting themselves as a viable choice, but this only gets them excluded even more. On the other end, the Japanese, unaccustomed to functioning outside the context of group ensemble, mistake the American freedom of choice for "anything goes." For example, a university professor once told me about a Japanese student who came to him one day and said, "You will be my advisor." Trying to exercise his individual right to choose, and trying to be assertive—the Japanese are always told they are not assertive enough—he ended up overdoing it. Adjustment to each other's play in cross-cultural communication is tricky business, but an understanding of differences in decision making and the way they are expressed in American and Japanese interaction can make the two systems more communicable, and so give cross-cultural players a better handle on each other's game.

Team Stars, Borrowed Individuals

A popular theme heard every now and again is that the Japanese and the Americans are becoming more alike. Americans too work together in teams, and not all Japanese are the same—there are personal differences even among the Japanese. The Americans and the Japanese are converging, especially in the fastlane Business Culture, goes this theme. Nothing could be further from the truth. Although American teams and Japanese individuals are glorified as a kind of "reverse chic" in each country—that is precisely the point. Prestige in the counter-culture does not explode ideals; in fact, it often works to create a tension that makes the prestigious even more desirable.

For example, in the past two decades, American business has increasingly promoted team-oriented concepts: Teamwork, team players, team spirit. But financial rewards are still primarily individually driven. Members of a team are evaluated for merit pay separately, and it is considered unfair if one player's poor work severely affects the pay of another's. This contrasts with the actions of senior executives in the 1995 scandal involving Iguchi Toshihide at Daiwa Bank: Some resigned while others accepted pay cuts to take responsibility for the loss incurred by Iguchi. In Japanese business, one person's performance does affect the whole team.

In contrast, in American business, particularly capable individuals are star players held up before others as examples to envy or emulate. In the recent years of downsizing companies, financial compensation for the individual—rather than for the team—has been on the increase. For example, in two of the meetings I recorded between an American consultant and bank executives, a consultant discusses his proposal for cash bonuses to be paid out to individuals who help increase the bank's profitability. Identified as key players in the so-called turnaround, these individuals would profit from a competitive game of productivity and performance in which an individual of excelling performance reaps his or her own reward.

What's more, in talk, when people say so-and-so is "good" in business, they usually mean, "She's good at her job," not that "She's a good team player." If this were the meaning, it would have to be stated that way. The interpretation of a word without qualification is what linguists refer to as "unmarked," like the interpretation of "good at her job" from the word "good." A "marked" interpretation on the other hand, is conditional to qualification; "good team player" can only be understood by adding "team player" to "good," not simply from "good." The fact that the unmodified "good" means "individually good" shows the assumption that the individual is the unmarked norm, while the team is the marked variation.

The Japanese, on the other hand, often view stars as show-offs, and try to nip them in the bud. Major league pitcher Nomo Hideo's story is a prime example. Nomo had established a successful pitching record for the Kintetsu Buffaloes in Japan until he was set back by a shoulder injury in 1994. At the end of the season, Nomo asked for a multiyear contract, but Kintetsu refused, reminding him that multiyear contracts were reserved for veterans who had served out a term of ten seasons to gain free agency. Nomo then retired and was promptly recruited by the Los Angeles Dodgers.

When the news hit, the Japanese media were outraged. Portraying Nomo as an overweight brat, they said he was destined to fail. But striking out batter after batter with his tornado pitches, Nomo not only proved them wrong, but also became a hero in American baseball, which, demoralized by labor disputes and unproductive millionaire players, was badly in need of a moral boost. So here he was: The new kid on the block, a hustler and a star. In no time, the excitement ricocheted back to Japan, where the Japanese, now reconciled to the newfound fame of their homegrown player in a foreign land, cheered on their lost star from afar. Irony of ironies, Nomo could only be a hero because he left Japan.

A success in Japan is not someone who stands out and breaks apart from the crowd. It cannot be, as described by the CEO of a Japanese automobile company, "someone who gets the job done, but has a bad attitude."[8] Rather, a person's *shusse* or success is seen as resulting from an understanding of the workings of the ensemble, and a will to stand by others through thick and thin. Rewards and failures are experienced together as a group, not as an individual.

In two consecutive meetings I recorded, an American consultant selling a proposal of cash incentives for top performers has one audience that is American, and another that is Japanese. His sell to the American is much easier than to the Japanese, who repeatedly questions the basis of the proposal. "It is not a part of our management philosophy," he says, implying that the Japanese management is unlikely to endorse a proposal which gives star players extraordinary pay. For the Japanese then, the socially unmarked and sanctioned mode of relationship is the team player, while the individual is the marked variation.

But similar to the way the concept of teamwork is treated among Americans, the Japanese do portray the idealized individual—like Nomo—as an American with reverse chic. Such an individual is someone who is free of daily humdrum obligations, and the glamorization can be found in the images implied by the code word for the individual in Japanese, "my": My home, my family, my life. These words, written in English or *katakana*, the syllabary for foreign words, are intended to impart the feeling of a free spirit without the care of Japanese interdependence.

The ultimate incarnation of this "my" spirit is in the song, "My Way" found in almost every respectable karaoke bar. There is nothing like hearing an American sing, "I did it My Way," that enshrines the Japanese idolization of *my* independence. But like the one-night entertainment of "My Way," or foreign word borrowings written in English and katakana, *my* independence serves only as an accessory or a reverse chic that reinforces the notion of interdependence in ordinary life. Being fluent in English, singing "My Way" or being an individual is adventuresome, but it is also fabulously exotic.

This consistent treatment of things foreign as superfluous to Japanese relationships really hit home one day when I saw a tube of cheese labeled My Cheese on the shelf of a Japanese food market. Cheese is a safe product to put next to *my* because dairy products only made headway into Japan at the turn of the century, and were not really marketed widely until after the Second World War. A Japanese could then eat My Cheese and buy the fantasy of being an American individual without encroaching on fundamental Japanese beliefs.

But hard evidence is found by comparing the reverse chic to the principal ideal: The complexity of the latter far outweighs the former. Unlike the thin borrowing of *my* individualism in the Japanese communicative field, the American field has a dense description of independence, because the ideal, independent American is not just a free spirit who recklessly and selfishly goes for broke. That would be like a tennis player who hits the ball hard but wildly. To achieve the American ideal of independence, you need to be competent in exercising independence without costing others unduly. That is more like hitting the shots hard, and getting them just inside the line, consistently.

Similarly, the densely nested networks of Japanese interdependence show a more elaborate organization of grouping than the American concept of teamwork in business. Grouping in Japanese terms is not just about distinguishing between business and play. In the Japanese game, that would be like a player who can play back easy shots. To be skillful in achieving amae interdependence, you have to know how to count on others, while constantly minding the principle of others-first. That is more like a player who can play back any shot no matter what.

A strong individual, empowered by the right to exercise freedom of choice. A web of interdependent parts, connected in the sweetness of amae. Both varieties illustrate how communicators create the context—and the justification—for their relationships, and how these unmarked modes of interaction are the defining ones, at work or elsewhere.

Promises: Words on Paper, Sounds in the Air

At a section meeting of an international department in a Japanese bank where I once worked part-time, a senior manager advised us on how to close deals with Americans: "Odo odo shinaide" (speak without hesitance), he said, and move quickly by "*satto*" (obtaining a written contract). Reminders like this are common among Japanese managers, and accompany the shelves of books in their offices on how to do business with Americans. In an article called "How Not to Lose the Trade Wars by Cultural Gaffes," John Pfeiffer reports on a study by John Graham and Sano Yoshihiro. They advise Japanese business negotiators:

> We [Japanese] arrive at trust primarily through personal relationships, while they rely on lawyers to write tight contracts and settle disputes. We strongly recommend American-style written contracts with Japanese jurisdiction. The written contract is your only assurance of compliance.[9]

A warning well appreciated by the Japanese, it is surprising to an American attorney building his defense for a law suit against the Japanese bank in which he is employed. "Of course you need contracts," he says. "How else can you do business?"

Here's how: Not all of Japanese business is written down, and written contracts play different roles in American and Japanese businesses. In American business, a contract is a kind of promissory note: A guarantee that the substance of talk negotiated and agreed upon is now really going to happen. Since a contract means a legally bound outcome in American terms, it is in the interest of the players involved to secure one. For Americans, contracts are the most explicit form of individual ownership—indeed, American contracts are descended from the English who primarily used them for conveyancing land ownership. Written in ink, such a contract was seen as a permanent, definite and exact recording between individuals, intended to prevent fraud and perjury. As written forms began to outweigh spoken agreements in importance, the order of prestige in American communication increasingly became, in descending order: The written, the spoken and lastly the unspoken.

In contrast, in Japan, a contract is more of an after-the-fact, pro-forma report resulting from a kind of meeting of minds. Because what matters is the agreement, oral agreements are often honored. As late as 1957, the Tokyo District Court ruled that an oral agreement made between Marubeni Iida and Ajinomoto for 30,000 tons (1.8 billion yen's worth) of (undelivered) soybeans was binding.[10] Because the highest prestige is assigned to the unspoken, hammering out a clear written contract is not the point in Japanese communication. Instead, the goal in the Japanese game is to aim for the common hitonami (like others) background where individuals blend together in the group: The more distanced and subtle the speech and writing, the better.

The words "odo odo" and "satto" that the senior manager used in giving his advice on obtaining contracts are examples of the kind of talk-distancing employed in Japanese speech. The words do not literally gloss as "hesitance" and "quickly" as the translation above might suggest, but instead suggest these words in sound. Odo odo conjures up an image of someone going back and forth in hesitance, and satto describes the quick sound of the contract moving through the air. The sound metaphors odo odo and satto give the action the quality of an implied impression rather than that of definiteness sought in the words "hesitance" and "quickly."

Like the onomatopoeia "splash," "achoo," or "meow," satto is part of a productive system of sound metaphors in Japanese. In addition to these metaphor for sounds, Japanese also has a large number of metaphors for non-auditory experiences, like the visual "twinkle," and metaphors for physiological or psychological states, like a "banging headache" or doing something odo odo (hesitantly). Recently, a doctor of eastern medicine gave me another example of one when he told me: "Moo chotto *BOO*tto shita hoo ga iinja nai desu ka." What literally translates as, "Maybe you should try to be more in a state of *boo* [sound metaphor of a psychological state]," really means something like: Stop trying to rationalize everything, and think about nothing every now and then.

While English has its share of these categories of sound metaphors, their frequency and usage is much more restricted than in Japanese because they tend to give the general feel of childishness, as in bow-wow, ding-dong, yabadabadoo, or of slang, as in "he was ga-ga about her." In contrast, sound metaphors occur with proliferation in Japanese. Instead of "it's raining cats and dogs," for example, in Japanese, it rains *jaa jaa*. But it can also rain more lightly, *zaa zaa,* or very lightly, *shito shito*. Rain water can slide of a roof, *pota pota,* hit the pavement, *picha picha,* and kids can play in it, *pacha pacha*. Unlike American communication where sounds and spoken words are shadowed by definite, written words on paper, Japanese communication pays tribute to the impression of indefinite sound in the air over words, spoken or written. In business, the use of sound metaphors translates to a less explicit form of promising, which, like promises in a family, are often informally stated or even tacit.

Taking care of business in Japanese terms is, then, like taking care of a family. From within a dense network of relationships where the investment is for a longer and more fixed term than for Americans, physical and psychological space is shared so that teamwork is enhanced and decisions that bubble up from within establish a strong foundation for support. In American business, however, business and family are conceptually separated, as are individual boundaries for work.

Each of these modes of interaction is further echoed in communication so that Americans prefer to make business agreements between individuals explicit with a written contract, whereas Japanese prefer to keep their business alliances implicit by depending on their unwritten and assumed promises of give and take in relationships. With the boundaries of each communicative field now established in Speaker Talk and in Listener Talk, the rest is discovering how each game is played.

5

Open for Business

OPEN	EIGYOOCHUU (In Operation)
CLOSED	JUNBICHUU (In Preparation)
Precise States	vs. Fluid Processes

One evening in Washington, D.C., I remember walking by my neighborhood drycleaner and seeing the owner closing up shop. Inside on the glass door, she flipped the panel across so the sign that said "Open" then read "Closed." An American shop, opened and closed by a sign that says so. Thinking back to the signs in Japanese shops, I thought about how different they were: *Eigyoochuu* (In Operation) and *Junbichuu* (In Preparation) read those signs. A Japanese shop in operation or in preparation, with a sign that shows the process.

Shop signs are like talk strategies that tell you when talk is opened and when it is closed, when it is in operation and when it is in preparation. This is a chapter on talk signs hung on the doors of American and Japanese business conversations.

Talk About Talk

I was once in a study group with three Americans and two Japanese when one American, Karen, asked a Japanese, Yoshi, what three questions he thought were the most likely to show up on our comprehensive exam. Yoshi responded with a question, "Are we going to talk about the exam now?" Because everyone was still writing and not paying attention, Yoshi repeated the question, and Karen responded impatiently, "Yes, are you going to answer my question?"

What seemed to Karen like Yoshi's unreasonable refusal to answer her question was really a Japanese strategy of bringing up topics. Using a communication strategy I call, "talk about talk," Japanese players comment on their own talk or hanashi to address the process of changing topics, and note the transition of how what they are about to say fits into the ongoing conversation. Talk about talk can be as short as a sentence or much longer, especially if the topic is intellectually or socially difficult. For such topics, talk about talk often turns into what the Japanese call, "*maeoki*" (literally, "putting ahead"), lengthy preludes that qualify and introduce the topic. If such maeoki (preludes) are too long, the Japanese may be amused or annoyed at having to listen to the long lecture. But by and large, talk about talk and maeoki (preludes) are necessary for grounding a topic in Japanese communication. Like the shop sign that says, "*junbichyuu*" (in preparation), the Japanese need a period of time to get ready for a topic before the conversation can swing into "*eigyochyuu*" or operational mode. Like a volleyball before it is spiked, a topic is "set" in Japanese before it is launched into play.

Like other communication strategies, talk about talk is patterned and strategic as demonstrated in the following examples taken from a weekly *kachookai,* or section heads' meeting. This meeting is composed of three male bank executives, Tanaka, Ikeda, and Shimizu, men who are *doryoo,* or colleagues who entered the company at the same time. All three were hired from Japan's top universities, conforming to the standard hiring process discussed in chapter 4. As middle managers on equal footing, they share the talk in the meeting in roughly equal portions, and guide each other through an uchi (in-group) conversation intended to sound out current issues.

The goal of this uchiawase (sound out) is to gather opinions and ideas for decision-building in nemawashi (consensus decision making) which contributes to the decision that is ultimately circulated through the company in the form of a proposal. While it is now common to hear about nemawashi (consensus decision making), it is often difficult to actually see the process at work. By examining this section heads' sound-out meeting, we can see a piece of the operation in action.

The meeting begins with nontask-sounding talk. Ikeda, the manager I asked to tape the meeting tells the other two managers why the tape-recorder is there, and that I am studying American and Japanese business conversation. Because the Japanese bankers are currently working in the United States and have themselves experienced difficulties in American-Japanese interaction, the subject generates interest and occupies a good portion of the nontask-sounding talk at the beginning of the meeting, each manager sharing his own experience of working for a Japanese bank in the U.S. The managers then switch to more work-related topics, with a discussion on schedules and upcoming meetings, and finally conclude with a debate on the proposal for instituting an in-house financial agency at the bank, called Agency X. Each of these three segments takes up roughly one-third of the meeting time.

The nontask-sounding talk can itself be seen as a prelude to the more task-related talk, giving the impression of a long lead into what Americans would consider the "real part" of the meeting. To Americans, this meeting seems backwards, since the business discussions are towards the end, and items that would be considered "miscellaneous" are at the beginning. The linguist Toyama Shigehiko has found this organization to be characteristic of what he calls the Japanese "conclusion-oriented" pattern, and contrasts it to the English "introduction-oriented" pattern where important points are delivered up front.[1] Key information is often carried in the first or "topic sentence" of paragraphs and stories in English, but in the comments and the conclusion in Japanese.

Directing the conclusion-oriented flow of topics, talk about talk serves to segment the topics, and to guide the audience on where the conversation is going. For example, the first talk about talk in the section heads' meeting occurs at the end of the nontask-sounding talk to warn the audience of a shift in topic towards a discussion of schedules. The bolded text in the excerpt below is a literal translation, the rest, idiomatic.

1. TANAKA: **This talk is completely different,** but there's going to be another American regional meeting around August.

The second and third occurrences of talk about talk in the section heads' meeting clue the audience into a discussion on work-related topics, and on the proposal of instituting in-house Agency X. Again, the bolded text in the excerpts below marks literal translations, while the rest is idiomatic.

2. TANAKA: **The talk is gradually** veering towards work.
3. TANAKA: **I wonder if all that talk** about instituting Agency X **has completely fizzled out.**

As each talk about talk is signaled with the word **talk** (*hanashi*), the audience listens not only for an introduction of a new topic, but also how the speaker introduces it—vital information is carried in the way a speaker qualifies his topic. Listeners use this information in their *sasshi* (guesswork) interpretation to collect their own thoughts and to set up an appropriate contribution to the conversation. Talk about talk is, then, strategic in that it informs the audience on a speaker's orientation to a topic, which then allows the group to shape the conversation towards integrated positions and interdependent understanding.

For example, in (1) "This talk is completely different, but," listeners can sense Tanaka's apologetic tone in what he characterizes as an abrupt or "complete" move away from a discussion of pleasantries and on to more work-related topics. Likewise, in (2) "The talk is gradually veering towards work," listeners sense again that Tanaka feels regretful about pulling the conversation towards work-related topics. Finally, in (3) "I wonder if all that talk about instituting Agency X has fizzled out," listeners can guess that Tanaka is for introducing the in-house financial agency because he brings up the controversial topic despite the fact that he thinks discussions on the proposal may have completely fizzled out.

Talk about talk is a basic communication management strategy in Japanese. In organizing talk for maximum listener interpretability, talk about talk links otherwise disjointed topics of conversation, answering fundamental questions on topics like: "What are we talking about? And, what are we going to talk about next?" Talk about talk introduces topics, changes topics or starts new ones.

But more than just organization, talk about talk acts as a kind of sasshi (guesswork) umbrella under which communicators can hypothesize positions, thoughts and feelings and look at their own conversation in its entirety from the viewpoint of an audience. The writer Matsumoto Michihiro describes a strategy called *riken no ken* used by *Noh* actors of classic Japanese drama to mentally reposition themselves as the audience.[2] Talk about talk is a strategy similar to Listener Talk that allows Japanese communicators to eavesdrop on their own conversation so that they can play up their desired role as listeners, and maximize a desirable outcome in communication.

Name Your Own Deal

In studying the Japanese strategy for opening topics, I compared them to an American account executives' meeting made up of three account executives in middle management, Karen, Lynn and Craig, who also met on a weekly basis. Of the three executives, Karen, the person I asked to tape the meeting, is the most senior, followed by Lynn and then by Craig. Despite these differences in rank, each account executive has the opportunity to report on their own accounts, so that unlike the Japanese section heads' meeting where equality is established by a similarity of rank, in the American account executives' meeting, equality is guaranteed by a shared belief in the ideal of equal opportunity. Formalized in a written agenda, the setup in the American meeting differs from the Japanese uchiawase (sound-out) in which there was no agenda to prescribe an expected sequence of talk throughout the meeting.

Given this fundamental difference, it is not surprising to find that the American strategy for opening topics is vastly different from the Japanese. In the account executives' meeting, instead of easing into the topic with talk about talk, the speakers jumped right in, and named the topic they wanted to talk about. These topics coincided with the "deals" for which the executives were responsible, and so each began to talk about their own deal by naming it. The named openings of the accounts are shown below, beginning with Craig's three accounts, and followed by one each for Karen and Lynn.

1. CRAIG: All right first **deal** today **is Morrow.**
2. CRAIG: The other **deal** uh that I have been spending most of my time on, **is Courtney.**
3. CRAIG: The other **deal** that I've started to work on **is Phelps?**

4. KAREN: **Brentnall, is,** ah **a deal** that is being—has mixed reviews on the marketplace.
5. LYNN: My deal—**Hinkley**—it **is** a complicated **deal.**

As the executives open their topics by naming their own deals, each conforms to the formula, Deal = [Name of Deal]. Like a mathematical equation then, the word "deal" and the name of the deal are interchangeable on either side of the word "is" represented by the equal sign in the formula. When the key words in the formula are extracted from the sentences, they form the verbal equations as shown below.

1. Craig	deal	is	Morrow
2. Craig	deal	is	Courtney
3. Craig	deal	is	Phelps
4. Karen	Brentnall	is	a deal
5. Lynn	My deal	[is]	Hinkley
	It	is	a [complicated] deal

By using this verbal formula to name their own deals, each executive makes an independent claim as the owner of the account. But because an agenda backs the agreement among these communicators to let everyone have the chance to report on their deals, each executive is able to achieve Equal Opportunity Independence, an independence that occurs within the confines of the group.

A great part of the mechanics that secures the organization of Equal Opportunity Independence is, then, a written meeting agenda. This predetermined contract ensures that the playout will go as planned because it tells meeting members who is going to talk about what. What ensures a smooth and effective meeting among American managers is the division of labor made explicit through a written agenda that divides the talk, and distributes independence to each and every executive.

And That's Just the Beginning

For every deal named by Craig, Karen and Lynn in the American account executives' meeting, each also gives it its own unequivocal verbal closing: "That's it," or "That's all." These verbal formulae that serve as topic closings occur at the end of each round, so that Craig closes the first round containing his three topics, and Karen and Lynn both close their own rounds with a topic each. Here are the verbal closures.

1. CRAIG: **That's all** I have.
2. KAREN: Anyway, I don't know, ah **that's all** I've got.

3. LYNN: Anyway, **that's it** on the deal.
            And then, so I think **that's it** on the paper that we've got in the
            market.
            Yeah, uh so that—**that's it**—it's closed on our books for right
            now.

By completing their own rounds, each executive carries the responsibility for his
or her own deals to its rightful conclusion. Both at the beginning of the topic and
at the end, the executives mark their ownership with the conversational signs that
say, "open" and "closed."

When the account executives' meeting draws to a close, a final check is run
to make sure everyone has had a chance to talk. The joint closure takes the form
of what conversation analysts Emanuel Schegloff and Harvey Sacks call a "ter-
minal exchange," with everyone chiming in to confirm the last "That's it" of the
meeting.[3]

KAREN: **That's it.**
LYNN: Yeah.
KAREN: All right? I think that uh **that's it** for, do you have anything else?
          O.K. All rightie?
CRAIG: Nope.
          Bye?

When Lynn and Craig both acknowledge Karen's checks for the meeting closing,
the two "that's it"s put a period to the meeting, sending a final salutation to
Equal Opportunity Independence in Speaker Talk: Let each and every individual say they're finished.

Silent Shifters

I have a favorite excerpt from the Japanese section heads' meeting that I read at
conferences and seminars. Armed with a stopwatch, I time the eight-second pause
that occurred between two topics discussed in the meeting. Shown below, I read
it as an example of what conversation analysts call a "topic shift," and this shift is
out of the nontask-sounding talk that occurs at the beginning of the meeting and
into a discussion of schedules, beginning with the first subject of an upcoming regional meeting. As you read the excerpt (a literal translation), count out the number of seconds, or use the second hand on your watch if you have one since I can't
do my stopwatch act on paper.

IKEDA: Because in Japan it's a week at the most.
SHIMIZU: Mhm, it's a week.
→   **[8.2 second pause]**

TANAKA: This talk is completely different but, next time there is again going to be a regional meeting around August.

When I let my stopwatch run its course of eight seconds, by the third or fourth second, a giggle usually emerges from the audience. A few more snickers bubble up by the fifth or sixth second, and by the time I am reading Tanaka's talk about talk, "This **talk** is **completely** different, but," the snickers turn to laughter; deep and uncomfortable laughter; the pause is way too long.

There are two reasons why an American audience may feel uncomfortable with a silence of 8.2 seconds. First, when compared to the American account executives' meeting, the Japanese section heads' meeting has more frequent and longer silences. There was an average rate of 5.15 seconds of silence per minute in the Japanese meeting as compared to .74 in the American, and the longest pause in the Japanese meeting was 8.5 seconds, almost twice as long as the longest pause of 4.6 seconds in the American. This finding, corroborated by other studies, suggests that Japanese have a higher tolerance for silence in conversations than Americans—an implication that is consistent with the contrasting American and Japanese ideals of the spoken and the unspoken. What's more, unlike talk that belongs to one person, silence does not belong to anyone, and because everyone shares it, silence is the ultimate form of unspoken interdependence. For the Japanese, then, there is no rush to get out of a silent bonding. To the contrary, the goal is to stay united in making the ideal seem a reality for as long as possible.

The second reason an eight-second pause can feel long is because an audience listening to an excerpt of a conversation only hears empty silence. But for the actual Japanese communicators, silences demand the active listening work of sasshi (guesswork), and it is anything but hollow. In every silence, each section head is asking: "Is everyone getting this?" "Do we need/want to keep talking on this topic?" or, "Should we move on to something else?"

As another strategy of Listener Talk then, silent shifting not only reads meaning into the silences, but also requires active decision making in them. This contradicts the popular view that silence is a breakdown in communication. In Japanese conversation, silence is anything but a breakdown. On the contrary, the *kanji* (Chinese character used in wrting Japanese) "ma" (meaning space or pause) is drawn to represent the sun shining through gates, illustrating how implied communication can shine through silence.

In contrast to the American account executives who verbally closed off their own topics, the Japanese section heads jointly changed topics through silent shifters followed by talk about talk. But each silence is also a potential continuer, and communicators sometimes test the waters by resuming talk, and then immediately pausing again to get a more accurate reading. An example of this double pausing occurs in the section heads' meeting on a topic Tanaka raises about instituting a financial agency at the bank where the section heads are employed. At the point where the translated excerpt begins, it has become increasingly obvious

that the other two section heads, Ikeda and Shimizu, disagree with Tanaka's view
that instituting the agency is feasible.

IKEDA: That's kind of difficult, because the entire management practices
            of Bank X [the heads' bank] is dependent on [tied to] that kind of
            profit.
SHIMIZU: I guess it's a little difficult, that.
→   **[2.5 second pause]**
IKEDA: The resolution of that problem.
TANAKA: But in any event, uhm . . .
→   **[4 second pause]**
IKEDA: Well, so, the **talk** was **kind of** incoherent, but . . .
SHIMIZU: That's true.
IKEDA: It's gotten late so, we'll stop about here today.
TANAKA: Yeah, that's right.

When Ikeda and Shimizu each suggest their disagreement about instituting
the agency by saying how "difficult" the arrangement would be, the first pause of
2.5 seconds occurs. Ikeda then appears to finish a sentence by saying, "The resolution of that problem." Then Tanaka, presumably reading Ikeda's comment as
a signal to start back up, begins to advance his positive position on the agency.
Half a sentence later, he cuts himself off.

The second and longer pause then expands to four seconds, and Ikeda comes
in with a talk about talk, "The **talk** was **kind of** incoherent," which is a standard
Japanese expression for ending an interaction by downplaying talk. As it turns
out, it is an expression that is not only expected but necessary in this meeting because the final topic had become contentious. The subtext for "The **talk** was **kind
of** incoherent" might read something like: "That was just *talk*. No hard feelings,
right?" And the meeting ends when everyone chimes in to endorse this idea that
all is well.

In Nakano Yoshiko's study that examines the interaction of an American
scholar, Dr. Miller, with Japanese television executives, Nakano reports a similar
finding where Japanese television executive Yamamoto drops a discussion of Dr.
Miller's fees because the figure suggested by Dr. Miller was more than what Yamamoto had in mind.[4] Without resolution, such an inconclusive ending may appear unfinished to an American audience. But among Japanese, the possibility of
leaving a topic without resolution only says that the conversation is temporarily
closed and may be picked up in later meetings. In the case of Dr. Miller, a discussion of his fees will probably occur among the Japanese executives, after which
the agreed upon decision will be presented to Dr. Miller again. If the figure is still
below Dr. Miller's expectations, and he does not agree to the fee, executives are
likely to drop the topic once again until an agreement can be made. While logis-
tics of this nature have to be concluded sooner or later, other business proposals
that circulate a company need not ever be resolved. Instead, as Tanaka points out,
proposals can just "fizzle out."

Instead of topics that are opened and closed with spoken definiteness like those in the account executives' meeting, then, Japanese topics are processes in operation, and the space in between them, processes of preparation. Floating like a balloon in the air, in theory, any topic can be retrieved if caught in time.

For both Americans and Japanese, changing topics means opening topics, so a topic shift is a topic opening. But while American topics are closed and then shifted, Japanese ones are just shifted with talk about talk. A final difference, then, is that the American meeting ends with a topic-closing strategy, but the Japanese meeting moves the meeting to an end with an opening strategy. These strategies reflect a larger difference in American and Japanese meetings: While each American meeting is a self-contained unit of individual decision-makers coming together for negotiation, Japanese meetings are part of an ongoing talk-in-progress.

Home Strategies at Away Games

Communication strategies that make sense at home often receive bad press abroad. A frequent American criticism of the Japanese is about their alleged inability to "finish" their communication, a feature made more obvious in writing. For example, in his review of a Japanese-authored book on business, an American reader criticizes the structure of writing as one that is prefaced with preludes, and notes: "The almost total lack of introductions makes it even harder to read."[5] To the American critic, talk about talk is ambiguous; it reads like a prelude rather than as a proper introduction.

But while talk about talk may not name topic openings in an American-style introduction, it does direct readers through topics. For example, one Japanese author writing in English changed topics with the talk about talk, "If I may digress a little," then went on to talk about the digression.[6] Another author shifted topics by picking up from a previous one: "Speaking of unanimous agreement. . . ."[7] If readers and listeners look out for shifters rather than namers, they can interpret the texts or conversations as the Japanese do. Texts will then be easier to read, and conversations easier to follow.

Another Japanese strategy that gets bad reviews in away games is the use of verbal closures such as, "the last item is," and "in conclusion" as topic shifters. For example, in a cross-cultural personnel meeting between a Japanese bank CEO and an American senior vice president, the Japanese chairman adds three topics which he refers to as "one last thing" before he finally stops bringing up issues. In Nakano Yoshiko's study of an interaction between the American scholar and Japanese television executives cited earlier, she also reports three uses of "one more thing" by the Japanese executives following what appeared to be a definite closure on the part of the American scholar.

Another example of multiple endings occurred in an American conference I attended where a Japanese speaker delivering a paper used "in conclusion" twice. Following each "in conclusion" with a prominent pause, the speaker had actually used the verbal closures as a talk about talk to head a new topic. But while Japanese shifters can be used either to open or to end topics, American closures like "in conclusion" can only be used to end them. Because of this, an American audience hears the repeated use of "in conclusion" as a mistake. The speaker's paper appears poorly organized because the second conclusion sounds like a tacked-on afterthought.

In away games, a speaker is often evaluated by the away rules of the audience. But in interactive cross-cultural communication, two-way interpretations make for double-barreled misunderstanding. For example, increasing evidence from cross-cultural studies show that when the verbal meet the less verbal, the former end up talking more than the latter.[8] In such cases, each emphasizes what they think of as the most effective system of communication. For Americans, their emphasis is on the agenda. Addressing items serially, they raise items on an agenda until the problem is solved, or decisions about actions for the future are proactively made.

The Japanese emphasis, on the other hand, is to listen carefully to the ongoing conversation. Sounding out their American counterparts and making ample use of silences, they determine where the conversation is going. Silences carry a heavy load of decision making, and the Japanese need lots of them.

But such silences, for the Americans, are too many and too long; the conversation seems to lag without conclusion. Another item is raised in the hope of getting a move on. But the Japanese feel rushed along, and think, "What did we do to provoke that?" They then might return to a topic the Americans thought was already finished or use more silences to figure out what to do next.

To prevent such mutual frustration, here are a couple of cross-cultural strategies to try out—not as cure-all remedies, but as experiments in trading places. For the strategists of Speaker Talk, silences feel long because they are blank. Speakers have made their contribution, and they are waiting for the listeners to become speakers, and do the same. A silence is, after all, just the necessary lag-time for speakers to come up to the podium, and take the stand.

But what about employing a strategy in Listener Talk, and filling up silences with active interpretation in addition to the interpretation work that goes on during talk? Temporarily forgetting about agenda items, how about concentrating on listening during silences, focussing in on questions like, "Is the section head agreeing with this so far?" and monitoring for background reactions? If nothing else, the silence will feel shorter.

And, doing what the Japanese do in silences will make it easier to understand how the Japanese think, which may then help in hearing what the Japanese hear. Even if you do not or cannot reach a conclusion about an agenda item during the meeting in session, in the long run, you will have a better idea about *when* an answer might be forthcoming, and *what* it will be. This suggestion is often cited in business books by the maxim, "Be Patient," but effective cross-cultural communication calls for more action than that: It is the powerful work of Listener Talk.

Then, for strategists of Listener Talk, what about trying the strategy of "talking out loud" about what is being heard in the silences? I found an example of this in the work of a Japanese scholar writing in English. After a discussion of Japanese communication, the author writes, "I am wondering if I have succeeded in making the Japanese patterns of communication intelligible to you," expressing out loud a comment which would only have been thought silently in Japanese conversation. Talking out loud is helpful in cross-cultural communication, then, because listeners can actually hear or read what would have otherwise been an implicit and unexpressed thought.[9]

Another example occurs in the cross-cultural incentive plan meeting. In interpreting the American consultant's explanation of his incentive plan, the Japanese bank executive, Kamiya, speaks his understanding out loud: "So you're saying that. . . ." By verbalizing the guesswork that is going on in the reflective pauses, this cross-cultural strategy, like the intracultural strategy of talk about talk, allows Japanese to talk about their silence. It is an exercise for strategists of Listener Talk to try out in communicating what it is they are hearing.

Whatever cross-cultural strategy, the Japanese use of talking about their silence, or the American use of active listenership in silence, both could benefit from further talk on cross-cultural differences in communication. Most people become more sympathetic once they know you're trying to understand them, and it goes without saying that a mutual awareness leads not only to effective communication but also to better business.

6

Scoring Points

Once when I was playing in a middle school intramural tennis match against an American school in Japan, my opponent's coach told her not to play my game because playing against me was "like playing against acid." At the time, I had no idea what that meant except that it made my opponent, who was ranked higher than me, make more and more unforced errors. In the end, she was so annoyed she could hardly play at all.

I later learned that the style of tennis my opponent's coach likened to acid was really what he saw as Japanese tennis, a game which slowly but surely wore down a competitor, and ate away at their patience. For my opponent's American coach, this defensive game was unlike the one he taught his players, where points are made on the offensive. In such a game, players win by making winning shots, not by making their opponents lose.

Although the intention behind my strategy was not as insidious as implied in the coach's characterization, "like playing against acid," I now recognize the strategy that inspired him to call it that. It was true that I was taught a completely different game where the point was to break the opponent, either by well-placed shots to the opponent's weak spot, or by provoking an error. As my coach told me, "Kaeshite, kaeshite, mata kaeshite." Return, return, and return again.

In the game that I knew, players win by preventing the other side from making winning shots so that the more they lose, the more frustrated they become, increasingly seeing themselves as making unnecessary mistakes. After a while, like my opponent in middle school, the recipients of this strategy lose their rhythm and their game. Like the goal in many of the martial arts, then, this Japanese strategy brings out the weaknesses of the opponent, so that ultimately, opponents end up playing against themselves.

The talk on Japanese tennis courts reflects this defensive playing style, as the frequent cry, "Bankai!" illustrates. *Bankai* roughly translates as, "Let's make a comeback!" and is used as self- or team-directed pep talk when a player is losing. Another expression used under pressure is "*Nebatte*." Nebatte comes from the verb *nebaru,* meaning "sticky," making nebatte mean, "stick to it," or "persevere." An American player once asked me for translations to these cries, but when I gave them to her she looked puzzled. In an American game that is won by winning, rather than by not losing, cries like "Yes!" and fist-pumping create a more appropriate picture of winners rather than nonlosers.

Not by accident, this Japanese gameplan of winning by not losing shows up in many different courts. For example in trade, Frederick L. Schodt discusses the contentious issue of how Japanese gain market share.

> The charge was, and remains, that Japan protects its home markets, fosters its own industries through a variety of policy measures, and then, when its industries are strong enough, decimates targeted American industries by using a concentrated low-cost export drive to grab a bigger and bigger share of the market.[1]

While American companies focus on gaining their competitive edge, Japanese companies focus on not losing their competitive advantage, so that the point of the American gameplan is to stay ahead in the game, while the point of the Japanese one is to make it increasingly difficult for other organizations to stay in the game.

In conversation, the way Americans and Japanese make points in their own groups parallel these different strategies of play. Americans make points by trying to hit them on the head—ideally only relevant points are made—no more or no less. But the Japanese make points by trying to hit them back, deflecting points in conversation to position themselves as interpreters of conversational points rather than makers of them.

But the gulf between American and Japanese gameplans motivates mutual accusation. Like my middle school opponent's coach, Americans often view a player who scores points from the receiver's court as devious: Strategists who play like acid target industries for decimation, and eat their way to the largest share of the market. Then, from the other side are the equally confused accusations by the Japanese who often view the American game of brinkmanship as a form of bullying. In comparing strategies for making points in business meetings in Speaker Talk and Listener Talk, this chapter shows that there is not only more than one way to win a game, but also more than one way to keep score.

It's My Deal: Present, Past, and Future

The three members in the American account executives' meeting, Karen, Lynn, and Craig, continue the pattern of round-reporting on their own deals begun in chapter 5: The executives first talk about deals that are closer to completion, or where the outcome is most known, and then go on to talk about ones that are more complex, or where the outcome is uncertain. These are usually deals in their early stages, or ones in stagnation.

Likewise, the points themselves are organized internally, starting from aspects of the deal that are most known and ending with those that are least known, rendering a systematic ordering of points along a *present-past-future* timeline, where known present and past aspects of the deal are talked about before stating predictions about the unknown future. As the executives present their own deals, each presents a sequence of points that conforms to the format shown below with its corresponding time-line.

Point Sequence in Speaker Talk	
Point Sequence	Time-Line
[Topic Opening]	
1. Report current status.	Present
2. Give background information.	Past
3. Cite future action plans/options.	Future
[and/or]	
4. Predict eventual outcome/completion date.	Future
[Topic Shift]	

Craig, the first player to begin the rotation, illustrates an example of the routine point-sequence.

Example of Point Sequence
DEAL: MORROW   PLAYER: CRAIG

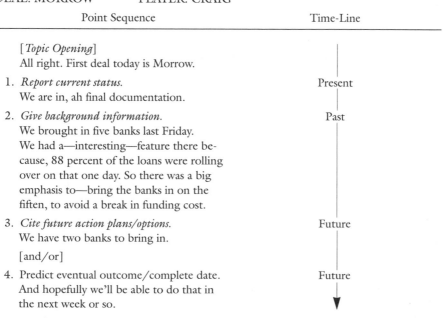

Point Sequence	Time-Line
[*Topic Opening*] All right. First deal today is Morrow.	
1. *Report current status.* We are in, ah final documentation.	Present
2. *Give background information.* We brought in five banks last Friday. We had a—interesting—feature there because, 88 percent of the loans were rolling over on that one day. So there was a big emphasis to—bring the banks in on the fiften, to avoid a break in funding cost.	Past
3. *Cite future action plans/options.* We have two banks to bring in. [and/or]	Future
4. Predict eventual outcome/complete date. And hopefully we'll be able to do that in the next week or so.	Future

[*Topic Shift*]
The other deal, uh that I have been spending most of my time on, is Courtney.

A similar sequencing along the time-line of Present-Past-Future occurs in weather forecasts in the evening news. Forecasters report on the current temperature and weather conditions (Present), then describe or show earlier weather conditions of the day (Past), or the weather on the same day of a previous year (Past). Finally, they forecast the weather for several upcoming days (Future). I have recently learned that some companies actually call a report on the status of their accounts, "weather reports," presumably because the organization of the reports are similar, and because it predicts future outcomes, which like the weather can be unpredictable.

Timeline presentations are also promoted in self-help books on improving communication and presentation. Like the weather forecasters, good presenters are advised to establish authority and credibility right from the beginning by saying up front what they know. Once the speaker gains the audience's confidence, she can then supply the background, and go on to predict plausible outcomes in the future. This timeline organization of points facilitates the communication among meeting members because everyone shares the expectation for how the meeting will progress. Meeting members may not necessarily agree on the content of discussion, but they do agree on the general model for how to present their deal. Such a model is the agreed upon style of good presentation, and any divergence from it gives the impression that the presentation and the presenter are disorganized and ineffectual. The way to score points in Speaker Talk is, then, by using the Present-Past-Future timeline.

It's Not Our Talk, It's an Example

Instead of capturing a point through sequenced talk, the Japanese executives in the section heads' meeting distance their opinions and comments in points made through examples. Such example-points are presented as hypothetical, which among other things, equips the speaker with a kind of parachute—if held to an opinion, the speaker can always say, "Tatoeba no hanashi da" (literally, "It's just for-examples talk"). Such a safety device is especially useful among Japanese businessmen who need to maintain good relations with one another. By positioning a point as only one among many, even contentious opinions can be dressed in examples so that personal relationships are not sabotaged.

A demonstration of example-points occurs early on in the nontask-sounding portion of the Japanese section heads' meeting when a discussion develops about the difficulty the executives have been having in working with Americans. Two of the executives, Tanaka and Shimizu, present the problem in terms of differences in corporate organizational structures in Japan and the United States. But Ikeda gets more personal, blaming his difficulties on a flaw he finds in the American character. In expressing his highly controversial position, he does so through an example. His contentious position is, then, presented as "only an example."

Citing a recent experience, Ikeda complains about an American accountant who goes on vacation despite a bad account that needs urgent attention. The verbal cues, **tatoeba** ("for example"), and combinations of the word, **yuu** (literally, "say"; equates to "kind of," "stuff like that"), signal the example-point and guides the audience to interpret the point as an example. Shown in bold in the translated excerpt below, the numbers indicate the way Ikeda organizes his points. As the excerpt shows, Ikeda actually makes two points in this excerpt. Example 1, the more specific point about the bad accountant is included in Example 2, the general point on bad accounts. Both these points are included in Example 3, in the group's general discussion of working with Americans.

The Bad Accountant (Translation)

The symbol ~ represents the approximate place the speaker makes drawn out sounds.

IKEDA: Yeah, but (**tatoeba**) **for example** [Example Cue 2], uhm~~ even in bank meetings where [we] discuss credits that have recently turned bad, uhm~~ well, in other words the credit has gotten bad so [I] think~ it's a pretty urgent meeting but~(**tatoeba**) **for example~** [Example Cue 1] the CPA~ uhm hired there, [just says] that [he] is taking a ⌈vacation⌉ next week, and so the . . .

TANAKA: ⌊[Laughs]⌋

IKEDA: . . . submission of the report ah~, is going to be late. And the result of that~, when (**aa yuu**) **that kind of** [Example Cue 1] announcement is made, uhm~ the banking groups~, [who are~] concerned somehow end up accepting [it].

[1 second pause]

And then~~ uhm~~ (**soo yuu**) **that kind of** [Example Cue 2] thing is just unheard of in Japan~.

[2.75 second pause]

That's (**to yuu**) **the kind of** [Example Cue 3]

[1 second pause]

. . . impression [I] got, but . . .

Picture this conversation as a circular sphere with Example 1, inside Example 2, inside Example 3. The excerpt shows how each numbered example-point reflects three levels of point organization so that the topic of "working with Americans," encases the general point about "bad accounts," which in turn contains the specific point about "the accountant." Each of these points is circumscribed by example cues. The "Bad Accountant" is surrounded by Example Cue 1 **tatoeba** ("for example") and Example Cue 1 **aa yuu** ("that kind of"), and "Bad

Accounts" is surrounded by Example Cue 2 **tatoeba** ("for example") and Example Cue 2 **soo yuu** ("that kind of"). The last example cue follows a pause of almost three seconds, and represents the final exit in Example Cue 3 **to yuu** ("kind of").

The cues, *soo yuu* ("kind of") and *aa yuu* ("kind of") are part of a series of words in Japanese beginning with *ko-, so-,* and *a*.[2] Literally, *koo* means "this way," *soo,* "that way," and *aa* "that way," but when put together with the word, *yuu* ("say"), they become words that describe a perceived distance of a point from the communicators. *Koo yuu* (literally, "this-way say") is something that is perceived as closest to the communicators, *soo yuu* (literally, "that-way say") is more distant, and *aa yuu* (literally, "that-way say") is still more distant. By using the distanced *soo yuu* ("kind of") to signal the general point about the bad accounts, and the even more distanced *aa yuu* ("kind of") to signal the specific point of the bad accountant, Ikeda pushes away his pejorative commentary on Americans and bad accounts together with his critical view of the accountant. Instead of a candid statement of how Americans are irresponsible, Ikeda combines cues to couch his opinion in an example, and to soften the impact of his words on the other two executives.

But Ikeda is not alone in pushing the negative talk out of the interaction. In the final stage of this example-point, everyone collaborates in banishing the negative points from the conversation. Such a collusion occurs despite Shimizu's seeming disagreement with Ikeda: "But (I) think Japan has been changing quite a lot recently," he says, meaning, "Japan, too, has gotten pretty bad recently. It's not just the Americans." Instead of challenging Ikeda's position, Shimizu's comment serves to switch the channel from a story about "lazy Americans" to one that might be called, "We are all victims of modern times."

When the other executive, Tanaka, agrees with this change in tack, Shimizu brings the three section heads back together again by pitying the entire group: "Those (of us) in charge have to pick up the pieces, so (we're the ones) (people) should feel sorry for." As Shimizu solicits commiseration from the other *tantoosha* (those in charge) with the phrase, "kawaisoo da yo ne," (us poor things, right?), he gets it.

By working together to finish the story as a *naniwabushi,* a sentimental Japanese story about pitiful characters, the executives reintegrate Ikeda back into the group, and regroup in their necessary assembly of kachoo (section heads). Like the cries, "*Bankai*" and "*Nebatte*" (Come on!) the executives keep pushing the negative points out of the conversation to maintain the desired level of interdependence, even as one member continues to make contentious points. In this way, example-points allow the Japanese to deal with the potential threat to group relations caused by different views expressed in talk.

Another conflict occurs among the three heads when Tanaka rekindles a controversial debate on instituting an American-based in-house investment agency in the Japanese bank where the executives are employed. Tanaka thinks it is a viable alternative to the current arrangement of using an outside agency that apparently never offers the best rates, and sends people off on a goose chase. An in-house agency, says Tanaka, would put an end to the trial and error maze of finding rates.

Tanaka begins the topic with the talk about talk, "I wonder if all that talk about making Agency X has completely fizzled out." Because the topic is controversial, Ikeda and Shimizu say they don't know anything about it, presumably with the hope that the topic will be dropped. But Tanaka pursues the topic further, and Shimizu disputes it, arguing that employees without commission are without incentive. The translated excerpt below, with example cues shown in bold, begins here.

Agency X (Translation)

SHIMIZU: So then~, so then how do you solve ⌈(that problem)?
TANAKA: ⌊Well so ⌈that . . .
SHIMIZU: ⌊So are you then say-
ing **for example,** all (you) can do is [laughing] release them from (their) shackles, from that part of (their) profit, or **something like** ⌈**that?**
TANAKA: ⌊Well··, uhm~
(it's) ⌈**something like that,** yeah.
SHIMIZU: ⌊[laughing] That's impossible.
TANAKA: Well (that's) impo⌈ssible,
SHIMIZU: ⌊Mhm.
TANAKA: But~, **for example,** that~ uhm~ if Agency X is instituted⌈, and (it) becomes part of us (this . . .
SHIMIZU: ⌊Mhm.
TANAKA: . . . organization), ⌈(we) can give (them) their profit say~
SHIMIZU: ⌊Mhm.
TANAKA: . . . **for example,** in the form of a "feeling," or **some kind of** profit of that sort, ⌈right?
SHIMIZU: ⌊Mhm.

When Shimizu begins to question the feasibility of Tanaka's proposition, he surrounds his example with the cues **tatoeba** ("for example"), and **tte koto** ("something like that"), and asks with ironic laughter: "So are you then saying **for example,** all (you) can do is release them from (their) shackles, from that part of (their) profit, or **something like that?**"

Tanaka then offers a counter-assessment, arguing that the employees can be subsidized by incentives other than profit, through various support mechanisms for caring, or what he calls, the "feeling" incentive as typically offered to other Japanese employees. This point is also surrounded by the cues, **tatoeba** ("for example"), **tte yuu no** ("that kind of thing"), **to ka** ("things like that"), and **sotchi no hoo no** ("things of that sort"). With these warning labels in place, Tanaka and Shimizu can debate each other's views without reproach because if at any point the threat to group relations appears too great, they can collectively push the example out of the conversation as they did with "The Bad Accountant."

Such friendly duels are also possible because example-points are coupled with strategies that further distance talk by reinforcing the idea that the opinion is only an example. The first of such strategies is the omission of pronouns that serves to diminish the presence of meeting members in the example. For example, in "The Bad Accountant," Ikeda leaves the pronoun "I" out of his opinion when he says, "That's the impression (**I**) got" in Japanese. By leaving the pronoun out, Ikeda divorces himself from the negative point of view expressed in the "impression."

Then in "Agency X," Shimizu leaves out three second-person pronouns when asking Tanaka, "How do (**you**) solve it then? Are (**you**) then saying that for example, all (**you**) can do is release them from (their) shackles, from that part of (their) profit?" By leaving out three possible references to Tanaka, Shimizu makes his questions sound less like a verbal assault, and at the same time makes Tanaka less tied to his opinion on instituting the in-house agency.

A clearly signaled strategy is one I have called "stretch-talk": A speaker stretches out sounds to show that he perceives the points as ones that are difficult to make. The stretches, shown as "~" in the English translation, call on the sympathy of other meeting members as if to say, "Go easy on me because this isn't easy to say." A third strategy is lowering the volume of the voice. Both Ikeda and Tanaka lower their voices when making their most controversial points. Like stretch-talk, a lowered voice shows the speaker's difficulty with the subject matter, and his desire to deemphasize negative viewpoints.

A final strategy that emphasizes Japanese point-making through examples is the appearance of agreement despite underlying disagreement. In "Agency X," Tanaka appears to support Shimizu's view that instituting the agency is impossible. Only after Tanaka seemingly agrees, and says, "It's something like that," and repeats Shimizu's comment, "That's impossible," does he give his counter-example. As seeming agreement, lowered voice, stretch-talk, and dropped pronouns reinforce the interpretation that an example is only an example, talk is distanced from the players so that a variety of points—even controversial ones—can be exchanged smoothly in the back court of Listener Talk.

But Listener Talk in cross-cultural communication is another story. Americans often interpret the Japanese style of example-point making as illogical, anecdotal or sometimes even pointless. For Americans who pursue Equal Opportunity Independence, communicators must play by the rules of timeline point making. Failure to do so is seen as poor presentation, a person inept at succinctly getting their points across. But for the Japanese who pursue interdependence, on the other hand, timeline point making appears ineffectual at managing the sensitive relationship among meeting members. "All they care about is the bottom line," say the Japanese, who misunderstand the American focus on the business-at-hand to be an intentional disregard of human relations.

What's more, because the gameplan for point making differs for Americans and for Japanese, both sides either miss or misinterpret the communicative cues that are signaled to show that a particular strategy is in use. When Americans hear stretch-talk for example, it often only confirms their suspicion that the Japanese are inarticulate or hiding something—and they miss the point that the hesitations may be an intentional cue to the audience on how to interpret the point a speaker is making. Different cues provide the context for a communicator's points, and it is only by knowing the context of such points—timeline or example—that we can begin to see the clues of how to understand what the Americans and Japanese are trying to say to each other.

Hanashi: Then There's Another Story

In a time before ball machines, my tennis coach used to stand on the other side of the net with a bucket of balls, and feed them one by one to my sister and me. We would hit them back for a while, and then he would stop and coach each of us on how to hit the shot we were practicing. The alternation of practice and lesson went on for the full hour of our lesson, ending with a wrap-up lesson for the day.

In the United States, the lesson-practice combination crops up often in the academic setting where learning is the main goal. At universities, there are lectures and hands-on practice, theory and practicum, or lecture and training/workshop. But in American business, learning is secondary to doing the job, and theoretical commentary occurs only in the margins of on-the-job training: in training sessions, workshops, and performance reviews.

In contrast, in Japanese business, wherever there is an *amae* (sweet interdependence) relationship—a coach and a student, a master and an apprentice, a boss and a subordinate—there is a daily dosage of lesson-practice. Even in the most routine business meeting, the student shows what he has done in practice, and the coach doles out commentary.

One such coaching session is a weekly, five-member clients research meeting in a Japanese bank in the United States where the primary objective is to report information retrieved to the *kachoo* (section head), Kishida. The meeting then serves as the gathering point of this information rather than as the locus for decision making or analysis, and each person says who he contacted or met in the preceding week, and who they plan to meet or contact in the upcoming one.

The clients research meeting begins as the section head Kishida discusses various upcoming *settai* (company entertaining). In this nontask-sounding portion of the meeting, Kishida's main concern is that the plans run smoothly, and so he coaches the meeting members by: (1) Informing them about who is picking up the important personnel in question, and where, (2) asking them to ensure a good turn-out at the events, and (3) asking them to give the number of absentees in advance. As Kishida outlines what is expected and what the junior members need to do, each prepares to go out and practice the instruction on the days in question.

Kishida acts as a pivot in the conversation that follows, ordering the presentations so they go from higher rank to lower. Then, after each report, Kishida tells a story. For example, the next-highest-ranking meeting member, Sonoda, reports on a visit to a computer game company, and Kishida tells a story that compares the CEO of that company with a CEO in another Japanese company. Calling the two CEOs geniuses, his implied point is that the account is top priority. More explicit may have been the coaching words: Make sure you give the company our very best care.

Then, when Sonoda reports on a second company called Pizza Movers which he plans to visit in the following week, Kishida tells another story. Pizza Movers has its holding company in its Hong Kong headquarters, and regional offices in other parts of the world. Comparing the organizational structure of Pizza Movers to the bank in which the meeting members are employed, Kishida reminds the junior executives that they are employees of the regional office, not of the parent bank headquartered in Japan. "Keep that in mind," says Kishida as he ends this story in which the implied point is about who the employees should formally present themselves as representing when interacting with clients.

Following Sonoda is a Chinese American employee, "David-san," who speaks fluent Japanese and English. David plays a role that politicians and political scientists jokingly refer to as "barbarian handler," bilinguals who are hired to "handle" the interface with the Anglophone business world. Many barbarian handlers are *kikokushijo* (returnees), Japanese who have spent part of their lives overseas.

David has visited with different members of the first two companies mentioned by Sonoda. Information gathering occurs at all levels in Japanese companies, and David is expected to gain information of a slightly different kind given his bilingual status. Each of the two mentions are also followed by Kishida's coaching, this time with reference to the special contacts that only David can make.

The other two employees, Watanabe and Tamura, discuss two companies already mentioned earlier. The amount of talk that is contributed becomes proportionally smaller so that by the time Kishida is finished with giving David advice, the meeting is 90 percent done. This means that the interchange between Kishida and the last and most junior employee is almost all lecture, with Kishida coaching Tamura on an elementary strategy of self-introduction. The meeting ends with a recap of the gist of the key lesson, as Kishida quizzes Tamura on whether he thinks he should present himself as an employee of the regional office or the home office.

"Think about what to say when someone asks who you are working for," says Kishida. Then before finally adjourning, Kishida fraternizes with the members of the group by confiding that he too has had a difficult time picturing himself in the new identity as a representative of the regional office.

Unlike the tips that we eagerly consumed from our tennis coach, the *hanashi* (stories) in a business context may sound more like *sekkyoo* (sermons) that are not always welcomed by the students. But whether a senior member of a company is worth listening to or not, Japanese employees still expect a boss to take the time to instruct. An absence of adequate direction gives the impression that the boss is *mendoomi warui*—that he doesn't know how to look after his relationships. This contrasts with the American expectation of autonomy—if an American boss constantly instructs his employee, it is not only intrusive, but also oppressive. Such a boss is breathing down the employee's neck, and likely to provoke the reaction: "Don't you trust me?"

But not so in an internal *uchiawase* meeting like the Japanese clients research meeting with its many layers of lessons. Beginning with task-specific instructions about taking care of valued clients, and ending with a more general lesson on wearing the right representative hat, the mini-lessons can further imply the company philosophy: Remember who you are, and take care of your clients. That is good business.

You Don't Know What You're Talking About

Part of the impression you make in conversation has to do with the amount of time you spend talking on a topic. You can show your interest in a topic by contributing, or you can look down your nose, and implicitly say, "No comment." Because talk quantity is more abstract, it is often ignored, but the amount of talk that a speaker contributes to a topic can play a great role in determining the weight of points delivered in conversation.

In both American and Japanese meetings, members talked in the amounts expected of them. In the American account executives' meeting for example, each executive talked most about his or her own deal. In the equal-rank Japanese section heads' meeting, all three members contributed to each topic in roughly equal portions. And, in the coaching session of the Japanese clients research meeting, the section head, Kishida talked the most, and the proportion of talk decreased with rank.

The players themselves subconsciously know they cannot veer from their own gameplan with respect to talk amounts. In the account executives' meeting, Craig knows he cannot lean back and say, "This is my deal, but I don't think I'll talk about it," unless he wants to look like he isn't doing his job. Nor could he hog the floor by talking about someone else's deal. Equally, Ikeda or Tanaka in the Japanese section heads' meeting could not talk one-sidedly through their contentious topics, unless they didn't care about getting a reputation about being selfish and egotistical. And, in the coached Japanese clients research meeting, the most junior member could not be the one to tell long stories.

The share each person takes in talk reflects a tacit understanding of the way power is distributed in the group. In the American account executives' meeting, each person talks about his or her own deal with little interruption, and this agreement on equal rights to talk translates to an understanding of equal shares in power among the three members. In the Japanese section heads' meeting, talk bounces back and forth among a group of middle-management peers so that the net effect is roughly equal talk shared in *each topic;* the group is held together through equal shares every step of the way. Finally, in the coached Japanese clients research meeting, where hierarchy, rather than equality is in play, everyone takes their apportioned amount; talk shares are determined by seniority.

The impression that someone talks too much or interrupts often is then not necessarily created because that person actually speaks more words than expected, but because of the sense that the *wrong* person is talking about the *wrong* topic. For example, at a recent dinner at a friend's house, we were talking about music, when I asked the hosts' fourteen-year old son, Paul, what he listened to. The answer, "Alternative stuff," provoked a flustered middle-aged pause followed by laughter, until Paul's father offered, "That's like Nirvana, right?" and tried rattling off a few more names.

But Paul would have none of it: "Dad, you don't know what you're talking about."

Wrong person, wrong topic, and even one name was a point too much. To score points in American conversation, and for them to be considered "the right amount," a person has to talk about a topic in which she is assumed to have authority, or one which no one in the group has authority. For American executives, such a topic is one in which they have a share of ownership, like a project or a deal where the more exclusive the outright ownership, the greater their right to talk about it. In a meeting where there is a collection of such owned topics, each person respects the right of others to demonstrate such ownership.

Japanese business executives in contrast base their point making on relationship, so that different strategies are used in relationships of equal and unequal footing. For the Japanese executives like the *kachoo* (section heads) on even footing in the section heads' meeting, talk is shared, but for the Japanese in a hierarchy like those in the coached clients research meeting, talk is distributed in proportion to rank.

Such differences in the effect of American and Japanese meetings are further accentuated by each group's different manner of delivering points. This chapter illustrated how the American executives followed a timeline progression for making points where the present status of a deal is supported by background information amassed in the past, and finalized by forecasts of future activities. In contrast, the Japanese executives made points through examples; among peers, anyone can make example-points, and in a hierarchy, the position of lesson/story teller is reserved for the coach. Like the tennis gameplan that scores by making points versus the one that scores by not losing points, Americans and Japanese each have their own means and motives for delivering points in meetings.

7

Support Network

In a land where business is family, Japanese see business entertainment as part of work. Unlike American entertainment, which is more often an additional option outside the required workday, Japanese entertaining, called *settai,* is obligatory and integral to an employee's life. The Japanese expectation is that a team member would oblige a boss's invitation to bond through such extra-work activities. A Japanese executive in an American auto plant was therefore disappointed to find that at five o'clock, instead of sharing a beer to show team spirit, workers went home to be with their families.[1] Asked an auto worker, "Why would you want to have a beer with your boss?" Used to a strong division between the "suits" in management and the union workers, it was unthinkable for the auto worker to share leisure time with a superior. Likewise, on the other side of the Pacific, an American expectation is unmet as an American beverage company executive in Japan finds himself plagued with after-hour company obligations. Says he, "It's *settai, settai, settai.*"

The ideals of independence and interdependence pull Americans and Japanese in opposite directions for expressing support. Japanese interdependence says, "the more of it the better," but American independence says, "up to a point, and then you're on your own." Supporting cheerleaders root on the sidelines of the American game, but robust shouters with bullhorns and bandannas almost steal the show from the players in the Japanese game. Either way, because support networks, though often overlooked, are the thing that can make or break successful communication, here are a few echoes of support in talk.

The Rhythm of Talk

I once got a call from Dan, a graduate student, and in the middle of the conversation, I say, "Hello?" because I think we have been cut off. But we haven't, and here is the rest of the conversation.

DAN: Is this a bad line? Should I call you back?
ME: No, it's just that you weren't saying anything.
DAN: But you didn't ask me a question.
ME: But you're still supposed to say, "'uh-huh, uh- huh," to show you're
       listening!

We laugh together because vocal feedback like "uh-huh, uh-huh" or what conversational analysts call, "back-channel cues," are the communication feature
Dan is studying for his thesis.

The Japanese call such vocalizations *aizuchi,* and the phrase, "aizuchi o utsu"
(hitting back-channels), images two blacksmiths hammering away in rhythmic
ensemble. A picture of Japanese rhythm in action, listeners chime in, "n, n, n,"
(uh-huh, uh-huh, uh-huh) to provide constant accompaniment for a speaker's
talk. The Japanese talk about aizuchi in everyday conversation: How a particular
aizuchi was read, how someone's aizuchi made someone else feel, and so on. By
contrast, although Americans use back-channel cues like "uh-huh," "yeah," and
"right," there is no ordinary name for these vocalizations of listener feedback in
Speaker Talk.

The contrastive significance attached to back-channel cues is featured in a
growing number of comparative studies that show that Japanese back-channel
more than Americans.[2] For example, in my study of American and Japanese meetings, there were only an average of six back-channels per minute in the American
account executives' meeting, as compared to nine per minute in the Japanese section heads' meeting, and ten per minute in the Japanese clients research meeting.
Then, in each of the cross-cultural meetings, the Japanese members gave twice as
many back-channels as their American counterparts. Playing up their listenership
and promoting togetherness, Japanese listeners indulged in back-channels because
it is a primary strategy of Listener Talk that makes listeners, rather than speakers,
the center of communication.

In contrast, because speakers are entitled to take center stage in American
communication, listeners are more conservative in their use of back-channels. In
the American account executives' meeting in which the executives reported on
their own deals, for example, the American listeners used back-channels to support an executive's introduction of his or her own deal. But once settled into
their position in charge, each speaker had full reign over their own deal. Listener
back-channels were then only used to recognize a change in speaker and topic,
and to confirm a speaker's in-charge status. This more spartan use of back-channels in American conversations occurs because in American terms, instead of
being supportive, overusing back-channels can raid a speaker's right to talk and
take command.

The different uses and frequencies of back-channels in American and Japanese
communication can make for cross-cultural hiccups like the one I was involved in

with Dan. Or, in the reverse situation, because an American speaker is left to speak for longer periods of time on her own, a back-channel is often misinterpreted as the listener's attempt to take a turn. When this happens, an American speaker may stop, only to find that the Japanese listener is suggesting the speaker go on. Then resuming, the process repeats itself, so that the conversation becomes plagued with jerky starts and stops.

Even more confusing to the American is the Japanese use of sentence-length back-channels like, "N: n: n: tashika ni soo desu yo ne:" (Yeah, yeah, yeah, that's exactly right). In cross-cultural communication, along with the use of soft no's, these seeming "agreements" have helped to earn the Japanese the reputation that they constantly agree, and then renege on their promise. Lengthy back-channels are misperceived as a sign of untrustworthiness because of a failure to see the double-track meaning in them.

The first track of a back-channel says, "I'm following you." But the second track supports the main mode of play: In Speaker Talk, listeners back-channel to agree with what the speaker is saying, but in Listener Talk, listeners back-channel to emphasize their role as interpreters. Whereas players of Speaker Talk are obliged to use and distinguish between back-channels of the "Yes, I'm following you" variety and those of agreement, players of Listener Talk need not. The Japanese send back-channels, then, whether they agree or disagree with what is being said because "Soo desu ne" (That's true/right/so) only means, "We're listening to you, and we're working out what you're saying."

Take for example the back-channels used in the following conversation between a Japanese industrial engineer and an FBI agent posing as an American company representative cited by linguist Roger Shuy, in his book *Language Crimes*. Based on the Japanese engineer's use of back-channels, the prosecution alleged that the Japanese engineer agreed to obtaining the plans, and that he knew that what he was doing was illegal.[3]

AGENT: You see, these plans are very hard to get.
ENGINEER: Uh-huh.
AGENT: I'd need to get them at night.
ENGINEER: Uh-huh.
AGENT: It's not done easily.
ENGINEER: Uh-huh.
AGENT: Understand?
ENGINEER: Uh-huh.

Shuy argues that the prosecutor's use of the above extract as evidence of illegal intent is misconceived for two reasons. First, the Japanese engineer may not have inferred that getting the plans "at night" was illegal—many Japanese work late into the night. Second, the prosecution's case rested on interpreting the Japanese engineer's back-channel, "Uh-huh" to mean "Yes, I understand these

plans are illegal and hard to get," an assumption which may have been appropriate for communicators of Speaker Talk for whom the right track is what the
speaker is saying, but not for communicators of Listener Talk for whom the "Uh-
huh" only means that listeners are carrying out the required work of interpreting.
In cross-cultural communication, players find it difficult to jump tracks, and continue to interpret back-channels as if they were occurring in their own track. Mis-
apprehension about what was and wasn't understood becomes the source of
harmful stereotypes so that Americans see Japanese as insincere agreers, and
Japanese see Americans as inattentive.

Different Rhythms

In the Intercultural Center at Georgetown University, there is a central atrium
surrounded by two floors of galleries that look down onto it. Standing in the galleries, you can spot people talking in the atrium, but you can't hear them. But I
have a friend, Ted, who claims he can always tell what language I am speaking by
the way my head moves.

"Your head dips every now and then, but it's more or less still when you're
speaking English. When you're speaking Japanese, your head bobs up and down
constantly in short jerky movements."

The head-bobbing occurs as a speaker makes her points, and a listener back-
channels, producing a Japanese beat founded on the underlying sound structure
phonologists call CV, or consonant-vowel. The CV combination of sounds in
Japanese produce a series of syllable-like sounds that consist of one beat, with the
exception of the sound "*n*," which occupies a beat of its own. On the other hand,
English not only has one beat syllables, but also one-and-a-half beat syllables.

The result is two languages that play to different percussions. The Japanese
rhythm, likened by the Japanese themselves to two blacksmiths hammering out
a conversation through aizuchi (hitting back-channels), and by linguists to a machine gun, contrasts with what linguists call the "canon ball" rhythm of American
English. Or, as Japanese language instructors often tell their students, what
Japanese is to rap (there is a folk dance called awaodori where the chants sound
uncannily like rap), American English is to rock.

Ted later learned the Japanese rhythm and some back-channels to go along
with it for a gag he wanted to play at an "International Coffee Hour" that hosted
a large group of Japanese exchange students. He wanted to test how the use of
back-channels could influence people's perception that you were understanding
what was being said—an especially interesting exercise since Ted didn't otherwise
speak a word of Japanese.

On the day of our performance, I began speaking to him in Japanese, and
with every head nod plus pause, Ted supplied one of his newly acquired back-
channels. After a few sentences, three exchange students gathered around him,

and one asked him if he had lived in Japan. He kept giving back-channels, and the prank worked for a few more sentences until a student asked him where he was from. The hoax was then revealed, but our exercise did show the tremendous power and utility of back-channels in conveying or giving the semblance of understanding in conversation.

What's So Funny?

In the nontask-sounding portion of the Japanese section heads' meeting discussed in the two previous chapters, one executive, Ikeda, offers his point of view on what turns out to be a controversial discussion on "irresponsible Americans." Raising the example of an accountant who goes on vacation despite "the serious matter of an account with bad loans," Ikeda argues that such an action would be "unthinkable in Japan." The other two executives, Tanaka and Shimizu, disagree with him, saying that Japan too, is changing; the implied message here: We're as bad as they are. As Ikeda distances his opinion through an example, Shimizu helps the managers regroup by pointing out a commonality among meeting members: that in the end, they are the ones who have to pick up the pieces as account managers. By invoking the image of "poor us," Shimizu refocuses the group on their interdependent relationship, while distancing their difference of opinions.

A similar distancing is collectively orchestrated at the end of this section heads' meeting, following another debate also described earlier on the topic of instituting an in-house financial agency called "Agency X." Here again, opposing points of view are expressed, except that this time, it is Tanaka who holds the controversial opinion, and Ikeda and Shimizu, who disagree with Tanaka, saying that such an institution would not be feasible because employees would be left without the motivation of commission. When the integration of the group members is increasingly under threat from the unchanging opposing viewpoints, Ikeda closes out the meeting, saying that they have run out of time.

In each of these disputed topics in the Japanese section heads' meeting, a listener laughs when a controversial point is made. As Ikeda describes the "bad accountant" who goes on vacation despite the troubled state of the bank of holding accounts with bad loans, Tanaka laughs. Likewise, when Tanaka mentions instituting Agency X in the Japanese bank, Shimizu laughs, saying with irony: So are you then saying, for example, all (you) can do is release them from (their) shackles, from that part of (their) profit, or something like that?

Listeners laugh in each of these controversial topics not only to show their uneasiness in the exchange of conflicting viewpoints, but also to signal back to the speaker that they have accurately read the warning labels attached to the contentious topic: Handle with care. Because the speaker and his audience are locked in agreement about how to handle the subject, they can maintain an interdependent relationship despite their debate. The Japanese often smile or laugh even when a topic is not funny not because they are trying to be polite as popularly advocated by some scholars, but because a laugh or a smile can show commiseration and empathy among communicators who need and depend on each other. Like other Japanese strategies, smiles and laughter demonstrate the need to get along given Japanese game rules, rather than sheer politeness.

This Japanese use of laughter contrasts with its use among Americans, who also smile and laugh to bond and show camaraderie, but the trigger for their laughter is usually something funny. For example, just before the closing in the American account executives' meeting, the group is tying together miscellaneous issues, ending in a discussion of a price war that is going on over the buyout of a rent-a-car company X. Craig then apparently echoes a phrase in company X's advertising, saying, "Although the price war is not extended to Manhattan," and jokes, "That's the soundtrack to X Rent-A-Car." The joke is that car rental companies in New York often describe great discount packages on radio commericials, but then end by saying that the offer is not available in Manhattan. The group laughs heartily at Craig's joke by chiming in with their own back-channels until Lynn tries to formally close out the discussion. Here is Craig's joke and the back-channels that occur following it.

CRAIG: Although the price war is not extended to Manhattan.
EVERYONE: [Laughs]
CRAIG: That's the soundtrack to X Rent-A-Car.
LYNN: Well.
KAREN: I know.
LYNN: You know?
CRAIG: Man!
EVERYONE: [Laughing continues for 2.35 seconds.]
KAREN: Try X Rent-A-Car!
LYNN: Yeah, uh . . . so that—that's—it's closed on our books for right now. And until, yeah, we c—ever hear again, from Chicago.

Immediately following is another joke brought on by Karen, who makes a joke out of her own question to Lynn that the deal is "off inventory" by saying, "I wish my mind would go off inventory." Everyone joins in laughter again to provide supportive feedback for Karen's joke. As the American executives joke to bond together momentarily before they disperse, the laughter at the end of the meeting also acts as a catalyst in breaking down the formality of a meeting so that they can go back and resume other daily activities. The joint laughter is, then, a mutually recognized signal that supports each individual as they go off into their separate spheres of work.

Although the Japanese also laugh for jokes, their use of laughter to signal uneasiness seldom occurs in American meetings, especially in those that are adversarial. This creates a problem in cross-cultural communication as described by a pharmaceutical sales executive, Gavin, who recently came back from a sales trip to Japan. This is what he had to say.

> I was O.K., but Gary [his boss] was going nuts with all those smiles and laughs. We just knew they were going to say "No," but they kept smiling the whole time. When we got back to the hotel, I thought Gary was going to lose it, and he says, "I hope you figured out what was so funny, 'cause I sure as hell didn't."

Knowing that the Japanese were smiling because they were uncomfortable might not have changed the outcome of the sales, but it may have at least eased some of Gary's aggravation at feeling that they were being derided the whole time. Making the interpretation less negative also might have maintained an on-going relationship with the Japanese company which could have opened up the possibility for contact on another occasion. But as it stood, Gary and Gavin misunderstood the Japanese use of back-channel laughter in the negative situation, and were consequently not only left without a sale, but without the opportunity for a future sale with a prospective client.

Taking Turns: The Ball Machine of Conversation

For me, one of the most satisfying things to do at the end of a frustrating day is to go hit tennis balls against a ball machine. It is a great way to let off steam, but the satisfaction also comes from being able to set a program, and then forget about the machine. It punches out the balls automatically, and you hit them back. A machine doesn't err, so you don't have to worry about it—or so you think—until that telling moment when one ball chokes up the entire system, and the expected shot isn't fired.

There is a ball machine in conversation that conversation analysts call turn-taking.[4] As with ball machines, we don't notice our program until it chokes: Someone doesn't take their turn when we expect them to, or someone talks out of turn. We call that an interruption. We think of our conversational turns as automatic because participants play by the same rules of a patterned program.

For example, research shows that the Anglo-American program is one that expects a relatively strict adherence to the chain, "I go, you go," with one person talking at a time. Comments like, "You've had your turn, let me have mine," and "I'm not finished here," show the view that each person expects to be given the right to an uninterrupted turn. A turn is a chance to demonstrate knowledge and credibility, and this distribution of power is exercised in the American account executives' meeting where the executives take the greatest number of turns in their own topic. In this meeting, the ball machine is preset in rounds so the overarching "I go, you go" is carried out according to the agenda.

Other cultural investigations of turn-taking show that Americans influenced by Jewish, Mediterranean, Arabic and African styles of communication take simultaneous turns that result in overlapping speech. These studies again show how members of the same group assess their own speech as involved and lively, but often get judged by Americans outside their group as chaotic and full of interruption.[5] But what remains, regardless of the particular background is that users of Speaker Talk strive to obtain talk.

In contrast, the Japanese ball machine is set to vary its program according to relationship—what matters is who is present at the interaction rather than adherence to a general program. The principle of this Depends-on-Who strategy described in chapter 3 regulates an interaction; if the conversation involves members in a hierarchial relationship like those in the coached clients research meeting, the program is adjusted. Kishida, the section head/coach gets the greatest proportion of turns (48 percent), and then goes down the line of hierarchy, from the most senior to junior: Sonoda (27 percent), David (15 percent), Watanabe (7 percent), and Tamura (3 percent). If, on the other hand, the executives are on equal footing as in the section heads' meeting where the three *doryoo* (colleagues) are of equal rank, turns at talk are divided into roughly equal portions. In either case, the person who is taking a turn at talk is carrying the burden of talk, not vying for its possession as among Americans.

When Americans and Japanese meet with their different turn-taking programs, two cross-cultural questions influence the resulting interaction. They are: (1) Are the players on the same side or competitors? and (2) Whose backyard is it?

When the players are on the same side and the relationship among players is relatively friendly, the outcome tends to be less problematic. An American takes the number of turns to which she thinks she is entitled to, and a Japanese shares the burden of the talk. Even though the programs are set for different goals, they can be mutually compatible.

But there is still the "backyard" problem. In an American backyard, a Japanese who is of a higher status than the American will inevitably hog the floor even in topics in which the lower-status American is better versed. This happened in a cross-cultural corporate banking meeting between a Japanese vice president, Tanaka, and an American office manager, Claire. In this weekly meeting composed of two Americans and two Japanese, of mixed rank, each participant used their native strategies for communication. For the most part, this did not pose a problem, until Claire began her topic about the new distribution of the filing system across divisions. Assuming the "responsible" Japanese role of carrying the burden of talk, Tanaka repeatedly took turns by asking questions that begin with "How 'bout . . ." and "Couldn't you . . . ," and ended up looking like a conversational bully.

Without realizing it, Tanaka's questioning derails Claire from her line of presentation, and robs her of her right to talk on her own topic. Unlike the executives in the American account executives' meeting who directed their own talk,

Claire is at the beck and call of Tanaka, chasing his questions even as she takes her turns. What's worse, when a Japanese male uses this Japanese strategy for trying to shoulder the burden of talk in an American backyard, it can be mistaken for male chauvinism. Through repeated experiences of this sort with high-ranking Japanese executive men, Claire learns to see the behavior as typical of an autocratic Japanese man. Because the higher-ranked person is expected to carry the burden of talk in Japanese conversation, Tanaka is likely to have done the same thing to a subordinate American man. But unfortunately Claire doesn't know this, so the cross-cultural blunder ends up bearing the further cost of being confused as a gender issue.

In another example, a Japanese executive, Itoh, operates in the backyard of an American executive, Sarah, in a cross-cultural personnel meeting. But this time, because Itoh sees Sarah as a partner on equal footing, he constantly tries to even out the number of turns each takes. For example, when he feels he has been talking too much, he "gives" Sarah turns by asking questions on topics that are officially in his domain. A similar "sharing the burden of talk" was demonstrated in the Japanese section heads' meeting where the executives of equal rank talked in roughly equal amounts.

Unlike Tanaka who felt obliged to carry the burden of talk on his own then, Itoh's questions are aimed at distributing the responsibility of talk. But while the effect is different from the previous interaction, Itoh's questioning is unfortunately still out of place. By asking Sarah to talk about a topic that she does not really consider hers, Itoh puts Sarah on the spot. Her responses show this, as she heads them with, "As you know . . . ," and "I believe you told me this, but . . ."

The friction caused by using a native strategy in someone else's backyard mushrooms when the relationship is competitive, and here is a typical example. An American presents a product or service to a Japanese organization. He waits to hear what the Japanese think. They don't say anything, and instead ask him questions that have already been answered in his presentation or in documents sent to the company earlier. The seller is confused, but complies, repeating himself. But the ball machine goes on and on, and the seller becomes frustrated. His conclusion: The people present at this meeting don't know what they're doing or what they want. And the buyer's conclusion: He'll never come back.

For Americans in a Japanese backyard, it is important to remember that the key to good business in Japan is an established interdependent relationship. Rather than hammering home points on an agenda to sell a product and close the deal, therefore, the ball machine might be better unclogged by taking your mind off the preset agenda, and focussing on the unfolding relationship that you are in the process of building. The idea is to concentrate on presenting yourself as a trustworthy person who is sensitive to Japanese interests. For example, ask a few non-sales-related questions about the company. By shifting your focus from product to relationship, you will be in sync with the Japanese expectation for interaction so that not only will your product get maximum presentation, but the same ball machine will produce a more satisfying rhythm than the earlier one that kept getting stuck round after round.

Americans and Japanese support different players in communication so that each is able to play their game of Speaker Talk and Listener Talk. By spotlighting independence, Americans let the individual speaker take center stage in Speaker Talk, whereas by highlighting interdependence, the Japanese give the supporting cast a substantive role in Listener Talk. The difference between these two focusses is apparent in a comparison of American and Japanese back-channels, which shows that the Japanese provide such listener feedback with substantially greater frequency than their American counterparts.

This difference alone creates an inelegant mismatch in cross-cultural communication between Americans and Japanese, as Japanese speakers stop to hear the back-channels they expect and don't get, and American speakers stop to let the listener in: Did you want to say something? But the result is more than just clumsiness; this strategy for support that is often accompanied by head-bobbing and smiles has gotten the Japanese into serious trouble as people who are always agreeing, "Yes, yes," but not really meaning it.

This chapter has illustrated that such misunderstandings occur as a result of the participants' unawareness of underlying differences in American and Japanese support networks. While Americans back-channel to recognize each respective individual's command over a topic and their successive turns at talk, the Japanese use lengthy and frequent back-channels accompanied by head-bobbing and smiles to emphasize the status of listeners who share the burden of talk in equal turns of talk among those on equal footing, and in proportion to their seniority for those in a hierarchical grouping. Often unnoticed among communicators or looked upon as "not really communication," support strategies like back-channels and turn-taking hold the key to a better cross-cultural understanding of the hidden differences in American and Japanese game plans.

8

The Truth about Teasing, Praising, and Repeating

Every person who is called to the stand in an American courtroom is required to recite a verse of the American ideal: "I swear to tell the truth, the whole truth, and nothing but the truth, so help me God." It is compact and complete, with a loaded sequence of words: Truth backed by God, told in a courtroom of law where justice prevails and rights are defended. Each concept has to clear the test for a legitimate trial; if any one of the items on the list falls short, there is a mistrial, a perjury, or a breaking of the law.

Truth, accessible to everyone, unites law-abiding American citizens towards an egalitarian end. But it can only be upheld by telling it. Even when the Fifth Amendment is invoked, a substitute speaker has to tell the truth. Prosecutors and defense attorneys battle each other in the court of *spoken* truth so that through speech the correct verdict is derived: Guilty or not guilty. Truth for Americans is a modern constituent of God, its essence attained only by talking about it.

Of course there are sworn testimonies in Japanese courts, but the sworn truth occurs without reference to God, without a jury, and litigations occur considerably less frequently than in the United States. The Japanese attach less significance to legal debate and often prefer to settle out of court in part because truth-telling is but one of many lesser gods, and too much bald truth can even appear clumsy. The expression *bakashoojiki* (literally, stupid honesty) reflects this view: nice but unsophisticated, someone who may be quite bright intellectually, but who is probably *kusomajime* (literally, shit serious). They do everything by the book. Since this is not always possible, advantageous or socially graceful, those who are too bent on honesty end up appearing *yoryoo ga warui:* Socially green and inept at getting a handle on the situation.

By contrast, a person who is *yoryoo ga ii* is savvy and adept at putting two and two together, quickly calculating the common good alongside her own stake in the situation. The yoryoo ga ii person judges what to say and what to leave unsaid, even if it means not telling the whole truth. Such a nuance of truth is *im-plied* rather than spoken because, unlike the words that allegedly capture the ab-solute truth in the American courtroom, the Japanese see words as approximate and awkward vessels for conveying multiple truths. Like the bumbling, yoryoo ga warui (unsavvy) people we run into every day, words are part of the inefficient but necessary equipment for players in Japanese communication, so it is up to the players to use them in a yoryoo ga ii (savvy) way.

The fundamental difference in the way Americans and Japanese see truth is further reflected in each group's style of praising, teasing and repeating. Al-though each style makes sense in its own communicative game, the effect is twisted or lost in cross-cultural interaction as both sides misunderstand each other's motives. When this happens, the other side appears deceitful, and accu-sations of dishonesty become standard practice. While there is always the possi-bility of real and intentional deceit in business, this chapter examines American and Japanese styles of teasing, praising and repetition to show that many misin-terpretations occur because of a misunderstanding of each other's "truths" and the goals each strives to attain in communication.

What's in a Tease?

There is at least one joke in each of the ten meetings I studied, and the most prevalent form of joke was teasing. Both American and Japanese executives teased others in their meetings, but they did so for different communicative goals and effect. An American teaser was most often a male executive jockeying for a position of power in the meeting, while a Japanese teaser, though also male, was one who dared to show intimacy before others.

For example, in the risk-based capital meeting called to straighten out the figures of the bank's risky investments, Peter displays one-upmanship twice by teasing two male colleagues. The first instance occurs at the very outset of the meeting when another meeting member, Harry, asks what the video camera is for. I explain what I am doing, and then Peter says, "She read your performance review, and decided she wanted to videotape *you*."

By bringing Harry's performance into question before the entire group, Peter challenges him. It is a symbolic push on the chest that says, "What are *you* asking a question like that for?" If Harry is going to be a respectable challenger, he can't just whimper away, so he rises to the occasion, bantering back, "Most photogenic, that's what she means, out of all the people in the bank."

The scene for the second tease is set a minute or so into the meeting, when Satoh raises the issue of waiting for the missing member, Jim. Peter disagrees, saying they should just move on, and let Jim catch up. Satoh then agrees, but Harry asks who called the meeting. This is Peter's answer.

PETER: How do we want to do this? Jim is really—confusing us here by not being here. Why don't we just go ahead and pretend like he's here and make him catch up?

SATOH: O.K.

PETER: Wanna do that?

SATOH: Yes.

HARRY: → Wh—Who called the meeting?

PETER: → Jim and I just sort of did it toge—**I kind of did—and told him** that he and I had called the meeting.

Forecasting the answer, Harry's question, "Who called the meeting?" implies that they should start the meeting with whomever called the meeting, so if Jim had, they would wait for him. The question also serves to put Peter's position of command in the meeting in question as it really asks: "Shouldn't you wait for Jim, the leader?" Peter responds, somewhat faltering at first, but then reestablishing his authority over Jim as he says, "**I kind of did—and told him** that he and I had called the meeting."

When Jim finally walks in, Peter then teases him saying, "Jim, you wore a yellow shirt, and were embarrassed to come?" Jim then starts off by attempting to give a reason for his tardiness, and then jokes back. But by this time, Peter, with a foothold already established in the meeting, is way ahead of the game. As the exchange below shows, Jim's tardiness has cost him the command position in the meeting.

PETER: Jim, you wore a yellow shirt, and were embarrassed to come?

JIM: That's correct. That's the way I was, having, I was having lunch with somebody and . . . [Noise of moving around]
→ You don't want me to sit with my back to the camera?

HAYASHI: No, O.K.?
[Palm facing up, gestures for Jim to sit at the other end of the table, directly facing the camera, and next to Peter]

PETER: → No. You stay right there.

JIM: [Stays where he is] This is good. Right here.

As Peter's joke about Jim's shirt serves to reprimand him for being late, it also provides the rationale for his exclusive position as the leader of the meeting. By saying, "You stay right there," Peter eliminates the potential of sharing leadership with Jim, and secures his position as the unequivocal leader by reason of first-come, first-lead: His position at the head of the table is symbolic of his position in the group. Ordering Jim to "stay right there," with his back to the camera, Peter designates Jim to a position of participation only.

Deborah Tannen describes the kind of verbal competition illustrated in the risk-based capital meeting as more characteristic of men's interaction than women's.[1] And, in her study of friends talking, Tannen found that "all the conversations between young boys (and none between girls) had numerous examples of teasing and mock attack."[2] As a one-upmanship contest that underscores the victorious individual, this form of "mock attack" teasing also appears to be more characteristic of Speaker Talk than Listener Talk.

Here's why: The teasing that occurs in Listener Talk is entirely different, and is accomplished by showing a greater degree of intimacy than what is considered appropriate in a given situation. Two examples occur in the Japanese CEO's section heads' meeting, a weekly meeting where ten section heads inform the CEO of the bank's current happenings. In this meeting, the first tease is sparked by the CEO, Kondo, who lights up a cigarette during the meeting. A section head, Satoh, who is closest to the door, goes out to get him an ashtray, and then on his return, makes as if he is informing me, but loudly proclaims: "Koko kinen desu kara." (Just so you know, this is a non-smoking area). Kondo laughs and smokes away. By pointing out the breaking of a regulation which in theory was made by the principal decision maker, Kondo himself, Satoh dares in front of the entire group to step across the limits of a hierarchical boundary to poke fun at the CEO.

The second instance of a tease occurs when a newcomer makes a late entry into the meeting, and Kondo takes the break as an opportunity to introduce me to the ten section heads present. His description of our relationship is intimate as he explains that he knew me when I was a little girl in primary school. "You haven't changed that much since then," he teases, "with your *okappa* (bob) haircut and all." (*Kappa* are mythical half-frog, half-human creatures that live in rivers. The bob haircut is named after these friendly river creatures because they have a fringe that goes all the way around their head.)

Then commenting that we haven't seen each other in over twenty years, Kondo remarks, "Not since my early thirties." He then asks, "I've changed, haven't I?" inviting me to tease back.

I take him up on it, and aiming at the same level of intimacy, I tell him he is much thinner now. The Japanese often discuss physical appearances to gauge time spent apart, and to bring back a rapid sense of interdependence through intimacy. Such intimacy, like that between Kondo and me, is not always private, but shared with other group members to foster more interdependence.

Another section head, Kishida, builds on this expanding circle of intimacy, and submits his own tease: "Wasn't that also the time when you were the most serious and hard working?" Working within the format of the tease—people then and now—Kishida mocks Kondo's character. By portraying Kondo as a serious and hardworking man before, Kishida implies that he is by comparison a lazy person now. This negative image is implicit rather than stated in the tease, which not only makes the tease more gentle, but also gives it the quality of an inside joke through which meeting members can bond in common intimacy. The collaborative teasing is brought to a close when everyone joins in to laugh, and Kondo makes the final self-tease to say that he wasn't that serious then, either.

Japanese teasing, then, pushes the limits on what is ordinarily considered "proper conduct," and says, "Look, we're so close, we can even take a few stabs at each other and it won't hurt." This metaphor of intimacy as the absence of physical pain despite injury recurs in Japanese; notably for example, in an expression that describes a father's love for his child: "It wouldn't even hurt if you put the child in his eye."

But teasing has its limits, and it is especially tricky because there is only a hair's difference between a *hiyakashi* (a tease) and an *iyami* (a hurtful, sarcastic remark). What's more, in cross-cultural terms, teasing has different effects in communication because it is used in different circumstances. Among male business colleagues for example, American teasing has more explicit "bite" than the shadowed messages carried in Japanese teasing because the teasing that occurs among American businessmen is often to establish status, while the teasing that occurs among Japanese businessmen is to expose greater than expected levels of intimacy.

Because both sides expect and grasp most easily their own style of teasing, and because each type of teasing has the potential to be interpreted negatively, teasing in cross-cultural communication is often lethal. Japanese often find the American jockeying for power selfish and inconsiderate: They're always promoting themselves. On the other hand, Americans often feel put down by Japanese who tease them about their appearance and character. An American friend once confided that she was saddened by her relationship with another Japanese, saying, "We used to be really close, but now she's always cutting me down." My guess is that the combination of the Japanese style of teasing and the American misinterpretation of it as a "cutdown" confused the fact that the two friends were probably closer than ever. A professor of communication, Thomas Kochman, writes about a similar misunderstanding that often takes places between African Americans and European Americans where African American teasing is misinterpreted by European Americans as a serious verbal assault.[3]

Such misunderstandings occur because among European Americans, intimacy is often expressed in praises rather than in teasing. But as I describe below, it is not just a case of substituting one for the other because each communicative field—American and Japanese—constructs intimacy in its own terms.

Praised to Death

Recognition is an important ritual in American interaction. At the Oscar Awards Ceremony for example, financial and emotional support is acknowledged in part because it is an obligatory ritual. The Japanese are often impressed by American plaques with names of donors and sponsors put alongside art or an erected building not only because the practice of donations and private grants are less common in Japan, but also because the recognition given to individuals jumps out at them as something extraordinary. Recognition for Americans is a way of saying, "You have recognized me as an individual, and I too recognize you as one."

A standard way for Americans to recognize each other is through praise, and while this can be accomplished at a formally designated time and place, it can also be done in the corridors of everyday life. In the American bank meetings for example, the executives used many quick, shorthand expressions of acknowledgment as praise. "Great," was the most common form, followed by "good job," "terrific," and "excellent." All of these praises served to recognize an individual's accomplishment, however casual or formulaic.

Formulaic expressions of thanks and praise also occur among Japanese business colleagues, but expressions like *gokuroosama* (literally, thanks for suffering it out together with us) collectively acknowledge a group's sharing in the toil of a day's work. Because the Japanese understand the minimal social unit in terms of the group, praising others in your own group can be interpreted as praising yourself. The underlying difference in the ideals of independence and interdependence can then generate different frequencies of praise: Compared to Americans, the Japanese use individual praise about accomplishments much more sparingly.

In fact, so sparingly is individual praise used that the slightest elaboration of individual recognition among Japanese can often be interpreted ironically as inflated praise that makes a caricature of the puffed up recipient. Nothing showed this better than the 1992 money-and-mobster scandal where Prime Minister Takeshita was accused of using organized crime to stop the harassment campaign mounted against him by a political party called *Nihon Koomintoo*. The Japanese press called Nihon Koomintoo's campaign (which depicted Prime Minister Takeshita as a great leader with integrity and honor matched by no other) "homegoroshi."[4] Made up of the verb *homeru* (to praise) and another verb, *korosu* (to kill), *homegoroshi* literally means "to kill with praise."

Shortly after the scandal hit the news, I was at a reception where there was a discussion about the homegoroshi campaign. An American man standing next to me said he had seen character assassinations in television commercials where politicians ruthlessly criticized each other on their personal integrity. "Sex scandals, money laundering, illegal campaign contributions, draft and tax evasions. Slandering someone to death, maybe," he said, "but how on earth can you praise someone to death?"

The concept just didn't translate to comprehensible American English because praise in American terms is a good thing, and the usual complaint is about not getting enough. It is possible to praise your kids too much and spoil them, or to brown-nose by praising someone with ulterior self-elevating motives. But in both cases, the intention towards the person being praised, though crooked in the second, is not to slay their character.

Praise in Japanese terms is in general a good thing too, but it is usually packaged in standard expressions like "Gokuroosama" and "Otsukaresama," phrases that mix in thanks with praise for persevering through a hard day's work rather than for accomplishment. "Erai" (literally, great) and "yoku ganbatta" (you really tried hard) are also phrases of praise for persevering against odds. Overt and specific elaboration on accomplishments are less common in Japanese because it can skirt dangerously across the boundary of immodesty; overt praise for yourself or for your own group can easily sound like bragging, and overt praise for someone else can easily make you look like a brown-noser with a hidden agenda. Instead, extravagant praise about accomplishments is more commonly associated with a Japanese style of self-mockery. By making overly self-aggrandizing comments about themselves, the listeners are left thinking the self-praiser is so ridiculous, he cannot be serious.

African Americans also have a similar sort of back-handed humor, but whereas African Americans use self-praise for verbal play, explicitly twisting meaning so that "bad" means "good," the Japanese use the available communication equipment—grammar—to humor themselves and others. For example, in using inflated praises for others in Japanese, friends often use verbs with superior verb inflections to intentionally violate their regular, equal-footing status. A comparable example in American English might be a parent talking to their three-year old who has just thrown a spoon on the ground: "Let me pick up your spoon, your royal highness." Only in Japanese, the ironic reversal of hierarchy is more obvious because the hierarchical relationship is encoded in grammar. A better example might be the French use of the formal second person pronoun "vous" in place of the more familiar "tu" when talking among friends. While African Americans and other groups no doubt use ironic praising, the Japanese use it frequently, and with less ambivalence in in-group interaction—that is, praise about accomplishments communicated within a group is almost always ironic.

I learned about the difference between American and Japanese in-group praising when I was once invited to dinner by an Italian American couple; the husband was a banker, and the wife an attorney. At one point in the conversation, the husband asked me about his wife, "Wouldn't Carrie make a really good judge?" I nodded, and he praised further, "I mean she has such a great sense of justice. And she's *so* level-headed. I think she would make such a great judge." Luckily I didn't join in on what I thought was a tease because they both looked earnest. Realizing that the threshold for exuberant praise among uchi (inside) members such as couples is much higher in American communication than in Japanese, I was able to spare myself the embarrassment.

Extravagant individual praise in Japanese is dangerous because it can easily take on the tone of an *iyami* (a kind of sarcastic remark). An everyday example of iyami is a comment like, "Maa tottemo genki de taikaku no yoroshii ojoosan de rassharu no ne," (Oh, what a healthy and well-built young girl you are!) to a child who is obviously overweight. Among those who are close, even iyami can be funny in a twisted sort of way, but between adversaries, they are deadly.

Homegoroshi (praising to death) is a kind of strategic iyami (sarcastic remark). By making embarrassingly exalting comments about someone, everyone concludes that the opposite is true. And, by piling on inflated praises, politicians can mount a harassment campaign that praises their competitors to death.

Repeated and Parallel Truths

An old school of thought in education says that repetition leads to understanding. Old fashioned language programs were the ultimate example of this: Hours of repeating conjugations were supposed to eventually sear a pattern of grammatical logic into our brains. Most language programs have abandoned mindless repetition in favor of approaches that are oriented more towards meaningful communication, but the belief that verbal repetition results in comprehension is still popular, and is frequently used as a sales tool in American business—not only as a way of selling products, but also as a way of selling ideas.

Repetition is a common tool in business because by reinforcing a key message it makes it seem credible. When commercials repeat the message that their product is good, they sell you a piece of constructed reality so that if you buy the product, you have in a sense, endorsed their sales pitch, and bought the seller's fabricated "truth."

Of course most of the time, buying and selling is more than just seeing a commercial and going out to buy the product. Especially for services or products other than manufactured goods, the negotiations that accompany business are more diffuse, typically occurring in a series of interactions. One example of this is the cross-cultural incentive plan meeting where an outside management consultant, Brian, is brought into a Japanese-owned American bank to increase its profitability. Among several strategies for improvement, Brian proposes an incentive plan in which annual cash bonuses called "grants" are paid out to key players in the "turnaround." The grants hinge on the players' ability to raise the bank's return on equity (ROE) from the 1991 low of 5.5 percent to a market average of 14 percent by 1995. To sell his idea in the form of an incentive plan, Brian must win the consent of the bank management, but most critically of Kondo, the bank's new CEO and principal decision-maker.

But before his final presentation to Kondo, Brian holds preliminary, sound-out meetings with two executive vice presidents: Kamiya, Kondo's right hand man, and Sarah, the head of Human Resources. In these screenings, Brian must learn how to please both the American and Japanese interests in the bank represented by Sarah and Kamiya. Satisfying Sarah's faction is more straightforward because the American executives have everything to gain from the incentive plan. According to the plan, the players who do exceptionally well get cash bonuses at the end of the year, and those whose performance is average continue to get the salaries they have gotten thus far.

But the sell to the Japanese management is not only more important because they are the ultimate decision makers, but more challenging because they are skeptical of his plan. On the one hand, if the plan is effective, the rewards for the bank is great: increased profitability. But on the other hand, if the plan fails, the management would only have instituted a competitive scheme that could undermine productivity in the long run. At the very core of this downside argument is the bank's management philosophy that doubts paying out big grants to star players—particularly during a time of recession and the reshuffling occurring among the bank's managerial staff.

To overcome the problem of split audience interests, Brian sets two separate meetings with Kamiya and Sarah. In the cross-cultural incentive plan meeting, Kamiya begins by spelling out exactly what Brian is up against, telling him that Kondo will probably not feel comfortable with the idea of "giving exceptional, extraordinary payouts" in achieving the 14 percent ROE, despite the fact that "people deserve market level bonuses or long-term incentives." In the name of Kondo's "take the heat" philosophy then, Kamiya articulates the grounds for Kondo's potential rejection.

In response to this opening, Brian clarifies that the cash bonuses are only for extraordinary performances within the set five-year period of 1991–1995. Beyond that point, he argues, executives would get payouts only if they achieved even higher returns. But the problem of the amount paid out still troubles Kamiya, and he resists Brian's sale by talking about the incompatibility of high cash payouts and the management philosophy.

This is when Brian begins to craft a clever sales pitch centered on an argument of repetition differentiating "target" levels of performance from "maximum" ones. A "target" level, he claims, is an achievable goal in a designated year, but a "maximum" level is an extraordinary level that is most probably not realistically achievable. Alternately repeating the two words, "target" and "maximum" a total of seventy-one times, Brian stresses the performance level over the amount paid, giving the same incentive plan a more conservative—and hence, desirable tone: Grants are paid out if and only if there is an increase in the performance level; no payouts for zero increase in profitability.

Presenting the "maximum" sum as a dream amount that the bank would almost never have to pay, and contrasting it with the "target" sum that Kondo would regulate, Brian casts his proposal in the best light possible, selling the idea that to reject his proposal would be to keep the bank at the currently low ROE, and accepting it could only mean profit. The bank had nothing to lose according to Brian because his proposal, held together in repetition, was a no-brainer win-win scenario. That was the convincing pitch that Brian sold as "the truth."

The masterpiece of Brian's sale of this constructed reality is his avoidance of a hard sell, since he acknowledges early on that that would only serve to push the Japanese management to reject his proposal. Instead, Brian opts for a softer approach, couching his message in a repetition that convinces his clients to draw their own conclusion that they cannot afford to refuse his plan. As the buyers focus on the repeated key words of his incentive plan, they are convinced that they have arrived at their own understanding that the proposal is a viable option for improving the bank's performance. Brian's success in making a sale then is due to his ability to create truth through repetition.

Kamiya also repeats his counter-argument that represents the buyers' version of the truth. But his delivery contrasts with Brian's word-sell as he repeats his counter-argument in "showcased" examples that contribute to an overarching message.

Here is an example: Kamiya's initial skepticism towards implementing Brian's plan is accentuated by an apparently misleading presentation of the plan which makes it appear as if cash grants are paid out to executives who perform at the market average. As described earlier, a market average would be an improvement on the bank's current returns, so in this first instance, these executives would be rewarded with a cash grant. But Brian's incentive plan is structured so that the target for returns is increased across five years, so that eventually and ideally, the bank would be profitable because it would have edged above the market average. Executives performing at the average at that point would then no longer receive the grants.

Kamiya finds all this unclear in Brian's presentation, but instead of an explicit question where he might spell out the lack of clarity in words, he points to a dimension in one of Brian's tables and says, "*For example,* here, you would assume that the ten EVPs [Executive Vice Presidents] are average for the 175 [$175,000 bonus]." Giving a concrete example for his argument, and signaling it with the cue words, for example, Kamiya not only indicates exactly how Brian's plan is misleading, but also showcases the basis on which Kondo could reject Brian's proposal: Do we really need to make such extraordinary payouts just to get up to average performance?

Kamiya repeats this point—implicitly—over and over through showcased examples. Here is another example.

> **For example,** in the past, all they [the senior managers] were responsible is to generate assets, now, they will be told to generate deposits at the same time, sell trust products at the same time. And of course it will be additional responsibility, but it's not—they're not gonna do something that's revolutionary.

Brian finds important suggestions in this mock trial for how to take his presentation to the CEO, Kondo, so the repeated themes, though contrastive, serve a useful purpose in the end. But not all meetings have such happy endings. In the cross-cultural risk-based capital meeting, for example, two competing themes are repeated in an in-house discussion about capital that is invested in high-risk business activities. Composed of two sides with four American members (Peter, the leader, Jim, a colleague of similar rank, and two junior executives, Harry and Carol) on one side, and two Japanese mid-level managers (Hayashi and Satoh) on the other, the meeting centers on themes emerging from a general discussion of getting accurate figures on the amount of capital funds held by different sections of the bank, and how this can be brought about. But as the meeting progresses, the issue of obtaining "accurate" figures become increasingly problematic.

First, there are systemic problems such as obtaining an exact figure from dynamic funds, and programming a computer system to log these changes in automatically. Because the current system is less than ideal, manual adjustments called scrubbing are required after the program is run. All meeting members eventually agree that scrubbing is necessary, including Harry and Carol, the two that are directly responsible for running the program.

But as the meeting unfolds, a Japanese executive, Satoh, finds a discrepancy in the figures produced for the meeting. This in itself would not have been a problem if the only goal of the meeting was to agree that scrubbing was a good thing. But Peter, the meeting leader, is determined to set targets for the next quarter based on the estimated figures presented at the meeting. But Satoh and the other Japanese member, Hayashi, apparently feel that it is premature to set targets at this point in the game so they use the inaccurate figures as a showcase for their platform for not setting targets. Satoh, for example, states that setting targets based on the current figures is "like making a wild guess." Together with Hayashi, who offers the suggestion that each of the different sections come up with a more accurate set of scrubbed figures and a target of their own, such showcases occur eight times in the course of the 100-minute meeting.

At the other end, Peter repeats his theme: "Let's just take these numbers as a starting point—we'll have them scrubbed, but we can still set a target to get the ball rolling." This view, supported by the other American meeting members goes through parallel repetitions with the Japanese view until Peter tries to grind the repetitions to a halt. Voicing his frustration, he says, "O.K. I give up."

In the end, both sides compromise as the group concedes to set a temporary target until the next meeting when a new set of scrubbed numbers will become available. But while concessions are made in the interest of getting on with other commitments of the day, the disagreement held in repetitions in the risk-based capital meeting is not resolved. To make matters worse, although the meeting members were officially all employed by the same bank, recent organizational upheavals had begun to drive a wedge in between the American and Japanese staff. Because of this, even small differences between Americans and Japanese become symbolic of the general malaise in cross-cultural relations, as exemplified in United States–Japan trade talks.

In U.S.-Japan trade talks and in both the incentive plan and the risk-based capital cross-cultural meetings, it is not mere coincidence that the American side drives for target figures. Numbers can be assigned a restricted meaning, and for Americans who prefer an explicit form of communication, they are seen as ideal. Especially in cross-cultural communication, a common view is that because numbers speak for themselves, misunderstandings will be minimized.

The only problem is that Japanese prefer implicit communication, and mapping out target numbers—however tentative—often makes them feel as if they are painting themselves into a corner. This fundamental difference between the American preference for the explicit and the Japanese preference for the implicit is the overarching theme that gets played out repeatedly in cross-cultural communication. As repetition does its number on emphasizing each side's point of view, the conflicting arguments are lost to a destructive playoff, creating a dynamics of the kind the cybernetician and anthropologist Gregory Bateson calls, "complementary schismogenesis," where each side only gets louder and louder in insisting on their own version of the "truth."[5] To show how convoluted a misunderstanding this can become, I end this chapter with a memorable story of complementary schismogenisis in which I was one of the guilty parties.

Mismatch

When I was living in Tucson, Arizona, I joined a health club with enormous facilities and a wide range of services. Of particular importance for me was their tennis club, which not only had night tennis, ball machines and a great instructor, but also had a system called the "Match-finding Service." If you joined the service, you were ranked by the pro, and whenever you wanted to play, you called up the service, told them the date and time that you wanted to play. They would then look through their files to match you up with a similar ranking player.

The service always came through and found a player, so it was an especially good way to meet people when I was new in town. I looked forward to these matches in the Tucson foothills to help me unwind from the day. But the setup was far from perfect. For one thing, we always had to play a match. At the end of the day, I often just felt like hitting balls around at a leisurely pace, leaving competition behind. But since a match was the whole purpose of the service, I ended up playing every time.

The other blemish in the system was that the matchups were not always even. This was inevitable since the ranking was assessed quickly by the pro on a casual basis. After the initial appraisal, the players were responsible for adjusting their own level by saying whether the games were set at the right level, or were too hard or too easy.

In one of the earlier matches, I played a woman named Sally for the first time. On our way out onto the courts, she asked me if I played a lot. I told her the truth: I played a lot when I was a kid, and through college, but I had stopped playing for a while, and had only recently started back up.

She seemed satisfied enough with my response until the end of the first set when I won, 6–0. Sally then came up to the net, and said: "You lied to me."

Thinking she was just joking around, I laughed.

But her tone was earnest as she said again: "You really shouldn't lie like that."

And so I knew I was in trouble. But which of the shots that I called did she think I was lying about? "I'm sorry," I said, back-peddling over the mockery I must have committed with my laughter.

But she was really angry. "Don't apologize! Just tell the truth!" she said. "And play fair."

We played the second set, which I again won 6-0, but far from feeling happy about winning, I was upset that my opponent was accusing me of cheating. The only remedy to this was to play the first set over. So I asked: "Shall we replay the first set?"

"Look," said Sally now more indignant than angry. "Now that you have enjoyed your outright deception today, I suggest you tell the service that your ranking is wrong." And then she added in whiny, sing-song: "Don't—'I'm not really good'—people. When you play like you do, you should just say it like it is."

By the time I had realized my error—that it was not wrong calls that were making her call me a liar but what I had said before we started playing—it was too late to try to undo the misunderstanding that had been festering for the last hour. So I told the service to move me up a notch in ranking, and called it a day.

Today, a few matches later and with some distance behind me, I am able to look back and understand the mismatch that took place between Sally and me. In the tennis game, framed as a competition for Sally, answers to questions like, "How well do you play?" or, "Do you play a lot?" allow for the size-up of a competitor. It becomes part of the decision to get psyched up for a tough match, or to relax, and take it easy. From Sally's point of view, I lied, intentionally misleading her by saying, "I haven't played a lot lately," because to her, that meant I wasn't very good, which in turn led her to take a soft position against me. I had wrongfooted Sally even before the game had begun. And that is why, in her mind, I had lied.

But for me, saying, "I am a good player," is on par with saying, "I am the most beautiful maiden on earth." As discussed earlier, such a positive self-assessment for a Japanese not only sounds boastful, but borders on the ridiculous. In a Japanese context, it would either provoke laughter of a kind similar to someone saying, "I'm such a stud," or exasperation, "Who does she think she is?"

For the Japanese, modesty rather than honesty is the higher-order code of behavior. This does not mean that the Japanese value dishonesty, but more that honesty has to occur within the boundaries of modesty. That is what I tried to do when I said, "I played a lot as a kid and through college." In my mind, that was a clear statement of my ability: I took on a sport as a kid, and then played it for a decade and a half before my playing time became less constant. It was as close to the truth as I could get without feeling like a big-headed bragger.

So here is the mismatch in communication. American players, who aim for the explicit, operate in a field where honesty is the high-scorer: Say it like it is. But

Japanese players, who aim for the implicit, function in a field where modesty scores high: Say it without pomp. What's more, when the initial mismatch intensifies as players sense that something has gone wrong, a default reaction kicks in: When in doubt, apply more of your own high-scorer. For Americans, this means telling the truth by appearing up-front and frank, while for the Japanese, it is telling the truth by appearing to say it *hikaemeni* (with a certain amount of reserve). Trying to get a better handle on the game then, the Americans say it more like it is, and the Japanese say it with less and less pomp. But the different communicative goals are precisely what caused the mismatch in the first place, and each side unconsciously ends up contributing to the mutually aggravating spiral of complementary schismogenesis.

In trying to cope with the gap that exists between her previous understanding of my ability and her current one, Sally says, "You lied to me," to mark the first shift in our downward spiral. The point-by-point playoff of our complementary schismogenesis is shown below.

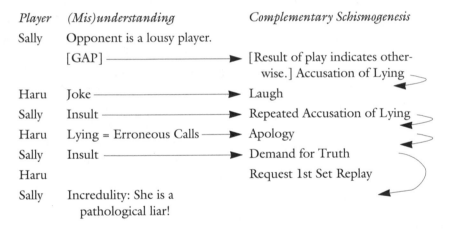

Player	*(Mis)understanding*	*Complementary Schismogenesis*
Sally	Opponent is a lousy player.	
	[GAP] ⟶	[Result of play indicates otherwise.] Accusation of Lying
Haru	Joke ⟶	Laugh
Sally	Insult ⟶	Repeated Accusation of Lying
Haru	Lying = Erroneous Calls ⟶	Apology
Sally	Insult ⟶	Demand for Truth
Haru		Request 1st Set Replay
Sally	Incredulity: She is a pathological liar!	

Like this mismatch, our self-umpired cross-cultural matches are ripe with the potential for miscommunication because of the differences in the way we count points: Some communicative instances count as truth, others, as lie; some as real apology, but others, hypocrisy. What counts as fair play for one seems like cheating to another. Then from repeated mismatches muddled with complementary schismogenisis come the unfavorable conclusions about the players themselves: a liar, a poor sport, or a sore loser?

In retrospect, when I think back to my interaction with Sally, I only wish I had the time to explain the contrasting values of honesty versus modesty, and how they play out differently in the American and Japanese communication. I would have explained too, that unlike Pinocchio, whose nose grows longer from lying, the nose of the Japanese goblin, Tengu, grows from bragging.

Americans and Japanese each have their own truths found in teases, praises (modesty), and repetition. The truth found in teasing among male American bank executives is about who is in control, but among Japanese men, it is about who has the closest relationship. The truth found in praising among Americans who are close to each other is about showing recognition of accomplishments, while praising among the Japanese has to occur within the boundary of modesty because it can easily end up sounding too flattering, a strategy sometimes used intentionally to assassinate a person's character. Finally, the truth found in repetition is that of explicitly verbalized words and numbers for Americans, but of implicitly showcased examples for the Japanese.

Truth is in the ears of the beholder.

9

Role Models: Working Man, Nurturing Mother

Language reflects our social histories—how we understand them, how we hope to continue or change the way we live, and how we set up role models to achieve our ideals. We seek out these ideals. Living in London, I have seen many an American come to search for his ideals in a British heritage, perhaps as landed gentry. The British caricature such Americans, mocking them as cultureless. But as we do when we use any stereotype, they overlook the complexity of such a search—that it is as much a confirmation of an American identity as it is a search for roots in the old country. Understanding the origins of an American heritage gives its researchers the means to evaluate how and why Americans came to be, and more importantly, an individual reason for being American. For what better proof is there than a story about a successfully bootstrapped individual—your great, great grandfather—who came to America, and made it. It's a story of how he left the social constraints of the old regime in favor of new social rules—competitive and fair ones—that granted wealth and prestige through merit rather than through the inegalitarian means of birth and heredity. Because paid work represented fairness in the new world order and distinguished Americans from the British, it became the American measure of success and social standing.

As Americans gained independence from the British, then, paid work also came to stand for independence. In the last thirty-odd years, American women, who had historically participated in unpaid work at home, felt denied their right to this primary symbol of American independence, and sought to remedy the situation by also empowering themselves through paid work. Like their male counterparts, American women grounded themselves in a system of prestige and reward set up by the founding fathers of America: Paid work is Equal Opportunity Independence.

With this backdrop, American women have historically been depicted as playing a game of "catch up." Women *gained* the right to work, to equal pay, and to vote. In such a story that depicts men as the trendsetters and women as players of catch-up, it is not surprising that American women have been seen as vested in secondary occupations in positions of relative powerlessness, and American men, viewed as the primary holders of power brought on by paid work. In America, this is how the working man came to be the role model to which both men and women aspire.

On the surface, the Japanese seem influenced by the same power dynamics in gender. Compared to men, women are less prominent in positions of paid work and public life. And, in contrast to men, women only got to vote after the Americans engineered a rewrite of the constitution following World War Two. But to draw superficial conclusions from these "facts" is bad translation because it assumes that Americans and Japanese have identical histories. Among other things, it overlooks the critical difference between their respective catalysts for change: Japan's social order was not brought about by declaring independence from a colonizer. Paid work was never symbolic of a self-motivated revolt to form a sovereign state. Rather, the symbol of work in Japan has largely stayed the same through time: Work, paid or unpaid, is seen as a responsibility of life where everyone has a role to play. Unlike Americans who participate in paid work to achieve independence through self-actualization, then, the Japanese play out their roles at work to belong in relationships of *amae* (sweet) interdependence, a concept centered on the role of a mother. In contrast to the working man in the United States, the national role model in Japan is the nurturing mother.

Overlooking the primary difference in American and Japanese views towards independence and interdependence, some feminists and pundits on women's issues have been quick to conclude that Japanese women, like American women, are powerless second-class citizens oppressed in a world dominated by men. In this chapter, I argue against this universalist position on women; it fails to see that Japanese women are different from their American counterparts, because each group of women has its own ideals about relationship and communication.

Mothers, Working Women, Housewives

In a survey among American and Japanese Catholics, one question asked who was the most important figure in the Bible, and the Japanese respondents overwhelmingly answered, "Mary" instead of "Jesus," as did the American Catholics. Among other things, the results of this survey demonstrate that for the Japanese, the quintessence of *amae* interdependence is motherhood. Perceived as the paramount form of nurturing and indulgence, the relatively exclusive amae bonding in the infant years is further strengthened in roles of "surrogate" motherhood, where women in various positions of early education are responsible for molding a child in its moral, social, practical and intellectual development. Both the earlier unconditional amae of a mother, and the latter disciplinary amae of surrogate mothers are Japanese images of power.

A popular reenactment of the image of the powerful mother is found in Japanese soap operas, where in story after story, mothers, portrayed as caring, resilient and savvy, take the center stage in a tale of amae. Repeating time and time again the heart-tugging word for mother, "okaasan," the melodramatic amae is meant to instantly move its audience to tears. Included in these *hoomu dorama* (literally, home dramas, or soaps) are of course, less-than-happy stories like the one I saw of a mother whose baby is snatched away and raised by another woman. But even in such a story, the point is not to portray the weakness of the biological mother, or the evil power of the baby-snatcher, but to reinforce the idea that nurturing is empowerment.

In contrast, in a society that holds paid work as an ideal, mothers are less favorably assessed because they don't get paid. American mothers often identify themselves as "just a mom" because to lack financial and other means of self-sufficiency is to be dependent, and being dependent—in the words of Timmy, the five-year-old son of my friend, Ellen, is simply not cool. When Ellen left her job as an attorney two months prior to her family's move back to the U.S. from the U.K., Timmy compared her to another mother whom he found glamorous. "Unlike you, mom," he said, "At least she has a job!" A better role model for an American child is a parent—mother or father—who has a paid job.

Respectable Japanese fathers obviously have jobs too, but unlike their male counterparts in the U.S., the jobs of ordinary *sarariiman* (literally, salaried man, employee) are usually not coveted by their spouses. Often discussed in commentaries in newspapers or in the lyrics of folk or pop songs, the popular metaphor for a sarariiman's (employee) life is that of a cog in a wheel: Dull, repetitive and lonely. In days where *tanshin funin* (employees posted away from their families) is common, it is not surprising that working men in Japan try to compensate for the absence of "natural" amae by recreating an emotionally interconnected environment in their workplace; a corporate amae (sweetness) that parallels the one they have been immersed in all their lives.

Japanese women also carry their share of more mundane, non-amae tasks, such as housework. But whether housewives do it themselves or oversee it, housework is seen as a part of daily working life. In traditional terms, housework was simply part of business, and like the Department of the Interior, a housewife's job included the management of the domestic budget. Today, household budgeting is still the domain of the Japanese housewife: She manages the budget of the family business in traditional-style families, or banks her sarariiman (employee) husband's paycheck, which she may later apportion to him as an allowance.

In a short October 1995 news spot on CNN about how Japanese families were faring in the recession, an interview on the streets of Tokyo showed a man complaining about not getting "a raise" in his monthly allowance from his wife. Asked how he coped with the situation, he said he usually tried one of two strategies. The first was to put his wife in a good mood so that she would be more benevolent to a request for a pay raise. The second was guilt. He said he would say something like "I paid for gas or our dinner out last week." Unlike American housewives, Japanese housewives control the household budget even if they do not have paid work themselves, inducing their husbands to envy them and jokingly call their privileged position "Ookurashoo" (The Ministry of Finance).

In her sphere of financial influence, the Japanese wife is also the purchasing department, from small daily buys to larger ones. A short while ago, I was in the local bakery here in London together with a young Japanese couple who looked like they had just arrived in the U.K. The man spoke better English than the woman, and he kept translating back and forth between the salesperson and his wife. When their purchase was finally bundled and totaled on the cash machine, the husband was in front with his wallet in his hand. But he moved out of the way so she could see the figures on the machine, and then the wife, fumbling through the unfamiliar bills and coins, paid.

This scene contrasted sharply with an experience I had in a garage sale in Tucson. Several couples debated over their purchases, each spouse okaying the other's buy. In one of these discussions, one couple decided they needed to withdraw money from a cash machine. This, too ended up in negotiation, and the agreed upon sum was withdrawn by the wife.

Although the wives ended up paying in both cases, the process, based on the assumptions about husband-wife relationships and division of labor, was different. In the ideal American system, husbands and wives have equal say for every purchase. This of course is based on the assumption that both parties have paid work (and are therefore equal), and the situation is different if one spouse is unemployed. In such a case, the spouse without paid work must get the permission of the spouse with paid work because the income belongs to the working spouse. A husband and a wife are equal with similar opportunities for independence, then, as long as they fulfill the terms of equality: paid work. And, this American belief in Equal Opportunity Independence is expressed by a negotiation of terms in verbal communication.

In contrast, Japanese couples play the roles expected of them, and as may be seen from the pains taken by the Japanese husband in the London shop to allow the licensed person to do her job, wives manage the domestic budget. Instead of operating under the principle of equal say for paid workers, the Japanese assume equality in a set division of labor where the wife manages the *uchi* (inside), and the husband the *soto* (outside). In the interest of maintaining this system, husbands often pay for "public" events such as an evening out. But the act often has more to do with keeping up appearances since the money paid out by husbands are usually drawn on bank accounts managed by wives. Similarly, many wives do work outside the home, but often downplay it for fear of others saying that they have gone off to work at the expense of their homes. Because Japanese women function in a society where morality centers on the views of others, like their male counterparts, they seek to be *hitonami* (like others), fronting a *tatemae* (appearances) that is often different from what is really going on.

I witnessed an example of this with a friend who habitually spoke of her family business as her father's business. She often talked about his difficulties of being self-employed and of running a small company, but then years later, when a question about her role in the company arose, she "slipped," accidentally letting out that the company was in her mother's name. In keeping with the Japanese protocol for the division of labor, my friend had presented the company as her father's when the family business was really her mother's. It made me wonder how many mid- and small-sized companies in Japan are actually owned by women.

So far I have described how American and Japanese women and men are grounded in different backgrounds that in turn give rise to different role models: for Americans, the working man, and for Japanese, the nurturing mother. But each symbol of power is also played out in American and Japanese communication, so that the ideal American communicator is the businessman who speaks up for himself and delivers his points clearly using Speaker Talk, while the ideal Japanese communicator is the maternal center of amae interdependence, someone who uses *sasshi* (surmise) to sense other people's positions and feelings in interaction, and then expresses them in implicit communication by using the talk-distancing strategies of Listener Talk.

In recent years, some scholars of communication have pointed out the similarity between Japanese Listener Talk and the American women's style of communication the linguist Deborah Tannen calls "rapport talk."[1] The styles are alike in two ways: Both prefer interaction based on group rapport over individual competition, and both can be characterized as women's styles. But these similarities gloss over a major difference. While women's rapport talk is the counter force to Speaker Talk in American communication, Listener Talk is structured on amae that is demonstrated most clearly in the maternal roles of Japanese women. Listener Talk—the main mode of Japanese communication—is borne out of the roles that women play.

This key distinction has historically been lost in translation. Equating Japanese women's talk with the American, researchers have been all to quick to conclude that all women's talk is powerless. The equation is unfortunately false not only because it assumes that power is absolute, but also because American independence and Japanese interdependence create different communicative fields for evaluating men and women. Each has its own terms of relationship, as demonstrated in the following conversations of everyday life.

Terms of Relationship

Dana Jones left a message with an operator at a Japanese hotel for her husband, Chris Evans, saying she called, but when Chris got the message, it read, "Mrs. Wife called." Instead of laughing at the nonsensical literal translation of the Japanese word, "okusama" (wife) into English, Dana found the message offensive because in her words, it invoked an image of "a helpless little wife." In her mind, "Mrs. Wife" signaled the related term, "housewife," which has now taken on a demeaning connotation in American English that invokes an image of powerlessness and low prestige. "Housewife" is shorthand for the stigma, "unpaid person," and to avoid the issue of payment, today, the gender-neutral word, "homemaker" is preferred.

The misunderstanding of terms was one thing, but worse was the effect of this misunderstanding in confirming prior preconceptions about the Japanese. "I guess they're just sexist," said Dana. Even more unfortunate was that the operator's message, though grammatically incorrect, was intended to show hospitality. In Japanese, it is more endearing and personal to use a word that references relationship, like "wife," rather than one that references the individual, like the name "Dana Jones." Terms that reference relationship sound more intimate because they include the hearer in the circle of amae interdependence, so the Japanese use them whenever possible.

Here is another example. Older siblings are typically referred to by terms of relationship—"oneechan" (Older Sister) and "oniichan" (Older Brother)—rather than by name. In fact, this principle of naming in terms of relationship is so central that the terms, "oneechan" (Older Sister) and "oniichan" (Older Brother) are used by those who are not younger siblings of the person named, and even to name those outside the family. Like "obasan" (Aunt) and "ojisan" (Uncle) that are used to figuratively mean "this woman" and "this man" respectively, "oneechan" and "oniichan"are used to mean "this girl" and "this boy" to invoke the kind of warmth of belonging that is associated with a family relationship. Although "brother" and "sister" are also used in American English, their use often takes on a more political or religious ring, and differs from the casual and everyday fashion with which it is used by the Japanese.

Instead, for Americans, names—especially first names—are more personal. Reversing the direction of the offense, a Japanese friend, Mie, recently told me about the experience she had at an airlines counter. To inform Mie and her husband that there weren't two seats left together because the plane was full, the ticketing agent said, "We won't be able to sit this woman . . . ," and then, flipping to the page on her passport with her name on it added, "Mie—next to you." In Mie's mind, the agent had failed as a service person. She thought that when she corrected her awkward use of "this woman" she should have said "your wife" rather than using her first name, "Mie." But the agent was being appropriately service-oriented in American terms because she corrected the impersonal, "this woman" to the more friendly first name.

Had this conversation taken place in Japanese, the problem would probably not have occurred because the term "okusama" (wife) can be used to refer to any middle-aged person to mean "woman of the house." If not "okusama" (wife), the attendant may have referred to Mie as "okyakusama" (passenger) which would then have shown her relationship with the airline company. To a Japanese, either one of these terms of relationship would have been preferable to the use of her first name, a term that shows independence.

The Japanese preference for interdependence is captured in a dish called "Oyako donburi" (parent-child bowl). The "parent" and "child" are actually chicken and egg spread over a bowl of rice where the chicken and egg are not separate, individual entities but stuck together as an undistinguishable blanket. Like oyako donburi, then, the Japanese use terms of relationship for both women and men because they seek connection in amae interdependence.

When Difference Isn't Worse

Another difference between American and Japanese communication is that Japanese talk is coded for gender. "Coded for gender" means that men and women not only talk about different topics in different ways, but there are specific words in talk that signal its user is male or female. One look at a transcription of speech, for example, is all that is needed to distinguish a Japanese man's talk from a Japanese woman's. Like all aspects of language, traditional distinctions change. For example, some teenage girls and young women use *boku*, a typically male first person pronoun "I."

But for the most part, Japanese is still coded for gender, and this fact alone has been the cause of a longheld misunderstanding: The Japanese language is inherently sexist because it distinguishes between genders. This hasty conclusion is false not only because it assumes that different means worse, but also because it assumes that women are deemed inferior to men.

The psychologist Kawai Hayao contrasts western and eastern fairy tales to show how western fairy tales use themes that consistently center around a male ego, but Japanese fairy tales use themes that center around a female ego. For example, a common theme in western fairy tales is one where a hero slays a dragon to save a maiden in distress, and then marries her.[2] But in Japanese fairy tales, marriage is seldom a featured outcome, and a more common theme is of a female protagonist who presides over other forms of life with power to create or destroy.

One well-known illustration of this is "Urashima Taro," a fairy tale about a poor fisherman who saves a turtle, and is rewarded by a visit to the palace of a sea goddess called *Otohime*. Three years pass in indulgence, when Urashima Taro begins to feel the need to go home. Otohime grants him his wish, and gives him a box, which she says should never be opened. But on returning to his village, Urashima Taro notices that hundreds of years have passed and everything has changed. Downhearted, he forgets Otohime's warning, and opens the forbidden box. A cloud of smoke surrounds him as it turns him into an old man.

Kawai informs us that this old favorite is characteristic of Japanese fairy tales that revolve around a female ego. But for a western audience, like the son of a Russian scholar, such a story was apparently pointless: "When is he going to kill the dragon and ask the princess to marry him?" he asked in the middle of the story. Without a maiden in distress, and without a hero to save her, the story was evidently hardly worth listening to.

Kawai's conclusions may be contested on the grounds that there are western fairy tales like "Cinderella" and "Sleeping Beauty" that revolve around a female ego. There is even "Pandora's Box," a myth that might be likened to "Urashima Taro" because it is a story about a box that is sent by the gods with Pandora as a gift to Epimetheus. Like Urashima Taro, Pandora too is forbidden to open the box, but does, and ends up unleashing a swarm of evils on mankind.

Notably, however, the genders of the characters in "Pandora's Box" and "Urashima Taro" are reversed so that failure is attributed to a woman, Pandora, rather than a man. Perhaps the contrast is not so much the gender of the ego, but the image of men and women presented in western and eastern fairy tales. In "Cindarella" or in "Sleeping Beauty," a man ultimately saves a woman in distress, and in "Pandora's Box," a woman sabotages the good will of men by her momentary weakness of curiosity. Men are not always central to western fairy tales but they do seem to be depicted as good and powerful, while women are portrayed as powerless and subject to foolish mistakes. The typical western fairy tale, then, contrasts with the Japanese in which both men and women are good and evil, powerful and powerless.

Like the reaction of the Russian scholar's son's to "Urashima Taro," an unfamiliar tale is confusing because the story does not follow an anticipated storyline. Linguists and cognitive scientists call this expected storyline a "script." In interpreting a foreign script, we translate the otherwise incomprehensible language into one with which we are familiar. But because two languages or two scripts are not identical, like translating using a bilingual dictionary, translating word for word without considering the sociocultural context only leads to a translation marred with misreadings.

Here's a recent example. There is a current debate in American English concerning the use of the masculine third person pronoun, "he," as the generic term for a person of either sex. Within the framework of Equal Opportunity Independence, a popular school of thought points out the injustice in a system that identifies men as the standard, and women as the variant. This school holds that the use of "he" is sexist—and here's the translation—any language coded for gender must be sexist.

Japanese is coded for gender, so for the sake of argument, let's say we use the same reasoning: A cover term that prefers one gender over the other shows sexism. Take for example, *watakushi*, the formal, first person pronoun for "I." The form is a variant of the female form *watashi*, rather than the male forms, *boku* or *ore* (and some men also use *watashi*), and it is also used by both men and women in formal speech. From this, we might conclude that the cover term "watakushi" is sexist because it uses the female form as the standard. The conclusion drawn from this line of reasoning often surprises those who call the Japanese language sexist because they expect the result to be the same as in English—that is, that Japanese is sexist with a bias towards men.

But this entire argument is the wrong script for Japanese. Personal pronouns like "he" or "she" define individuals, not relationships, the ideal among Japanese. Recall that this is why the Japanese often drop personal pronouns or use references that emphasize relationship instead. Japanese is coded for gender to a greater extent than American English, but because the relationships of men and women in each script are different, measuring each other's languages using the wrong cultural yardstick only results in superfluous findings.

When Difference Is a Minority

When people ask me what I miss the most about Japan, I usually say something like, "Certain kinds of relationships." When pushed to be more specific, I always find myself talking about relationships with women. Sociological surveys bear me out on the impression that there is much more same-gender interaction in Japan than in the United States. Such gender-grouping in Japan not only supports social and linguistic male/female distinctions, but also encourages gender-specific behavior. What's more, because men and women are evaluated in their own separate terms, being referred to as a "typical" woman or man—*onnarashii* (womanly) or *otokorashii* (manly) is often interpreted positively.

Such a frame of reference contrasts with the American, which evaluates gender distinctions less favorably, so that in some instances, it is thought of as best eliminated. Nowhere is this more clear than the workplace where American women have strived to be "equal" to men—equal opportunities and equal pay for equal work. In her book, *Talking From 9 to 5,* the linguist Deborah Tannen notes that women have achieved this to a great degree, but are still largely underrepresented in the power structure of management and decision making. Because women are in this sense "minorities" at the workplace, their actions become more notable, and sometimes, notably suspect. For example, in the cross-cultural risk-based capital meeting where members discuss how to get accurate figures for the bank's high-risk investments, Carol is the only (American) woman in a meeting of six (two Japanese and three Americans). Carol's minority status is quickly demonstrated in her conversational strategies: She speaks the least, gives frequent back-channels, and contributes only when invited to do so.

Then, thirteen minutes into the meeting, a meeting participant, Satoh, finds an erroneous figure in one of the printouts. Because Carol is the person who is directly responsible for the printout, she comes to the defense of the allegedly incorrect figure. At first, Carol thinks Satoh is looking at the wrong set of numbers. But when she realizes the contrary, she explains the discrepancy by saying she arrived at the figure by using a different method of computation. But by that point, everyone begins to doubt her.

CAROL: I think I've accounted for that. In the ones I did.
[2 second pause]
CAROL   See—
[2 second pause]
PETER: → Whatch—ch—ch—what—what's I'm not sure.

As Carol's pauses increase, she becomes more hesitant, and eventually seems to get confused.

SATOH: This doesn't add up. Two, three, nine, five minus three, seven,
           three, minus one, forty-six, is not? Two point seven one, right? It
           has⎡—this—three—. Three, seventy-three has to be
CAROL: ⎣It doesn't—doesn't work ⎡like—like that.
SATOH: ⎣Seventy-eight?
CAROL: → O.K.? I don't know—what we worked on.

Ten seconds later, everyone begins to agree that the numbers are wrong, and Peter does not mince his words in saying so.

PETER: → The—the last suspect lis—the suspect numbers are just *wrong*.
CAROL: They—they—they⎡'re actually I think reverse?
SATOH: ⎣Yeah, yeah, yeah, yeah.
PETER: A mirror image.

This joint evaluation of Carol's work which she herself admits is wrong has a devastating effect on her performance for the rest of the meeting. After a long period of abstention from talking at all, the attention turns to Carol once again, concerning a question about another figure. Carol is apparently the only one who saw the memo from which the figure was allegedly drawn, but just as soon as she begins speaking, she wavers on where the memo came from: "I thought it was from the real estate group?" She then also doubts her recollection of the figure on it: "Maybe I—I could have been misquoting those figures."

In rank, Carol is one of the two lowest among the executives, but more critically, she is outnumbered by men in this meeting who, as shown in previous excerpts, jockeyed for power by bantering cutting jokes about each other. In such a game of contest, all that was necessary to be considered a legitimate player was participation. Players contributing their banter equaled fair play, and the person who got the last word won.

But such a competitive dynamics contrasts sharply with "the style of community" that Deborah Tannen describes as the native style of many women.[3] Although Carol defends the error at first, she "loses" the conversation as she presumably becomes convinced that she is wrong. Carol's weakened credibility that results from her computation of erroneous figures becomes accentuated by her inability to participate in the confrontational style of interaction set up by the majority group of men. Her minority style then not only emphasizes her "mistake," but becomes the potential cause of the negative outcome: Being a woman explains the mistake. When difference is a minority rather than part of the majority, then, the majority often interprets the deviations and the tenor of the deviations negatively.

Mothering Bosses

Among management positions in the United States, human resources is one that is dominated by women. A number of scholars have argued that women, brought up to attend to the needs of others, are well equipped for managing people. The effect is what is commonly referred to as a vicious circle: Men don't pursue positions in human resources because of the view that such emotionally oriented jobs are best suited for women. Names for personnel further reflect a playdown of emotion: "Human resources" is preferred to "Personnel," and in some companies who prefer to omit the word "human" altogether, the distribution of work among employees is called "resource allocation."

Not so in Japan, where human relationships are considered the basis of business. There, human resources attracts a significant number of women too, but nurturing subordinates is considered a skill to be honed by male and female managers alike. As discussed in chapter 4, an inability to look after your own group is considered just as unprofessional as it is in America to be the one who is unable to leave personal and emotional feelings behind in the workplace. This contrast of viewpoints on professionalism was demonstrated in an experience I had when I was managing a Japanese language section in an American university. The group was made up of three women lecturers including myself, and six teaching assistants, three female and three male. All were Japanese.

When the problem was brought to my attention through the grapevine, I was surprised to learn that one male teaching assistant felt I unjustly favored another male teaching assistant over him. Presumably to communicate this more directly, the T.A. began dramatizing rebellions that soon began to affect the students and the members of the team. It was at this point that I asked various colleagues for advice on how to handle the matter. One female senior American professor told me to tell the assistant that he should just do his job. She saw the act as typically male and sexist: "He can't handle having a woman as a boss."

But my female Japanese colleagues, while acknowledging that his behavior needed to be changed, offered a different suggestion. They said I should try to spend more time with him so that he would not feel so left out. For example, I could go over handouts that he had made, or review grades of assignments he had marked, they said. It was obvious that he felt shunned, and like a child was staging "tantrums" to get my attention. Telling him to do his job would just be acknowledging these tantrums, they said, and more productive would be a gesture to show that he was included. Implied in this suggestion was that I was partly to blame for not giving him his due indulgence.

But a female American colleague told me that such an approach would violate professionalism in a number of ways. First, it would deny the T.A. the right
to carry out his job on his own; it would be an invasion of his job entitlement.
Second, it would breed mistrust by giving the impression that I was constantly
looking over his shoulder. And finally, the Japanese course of action would be
considered too emotionally involved to be considered professional. The T.A. was
an adult, and I was not responsible for his emotional well-being.

But my Japanese colleagues had a second phase of advice. After I had
coached him on how to improve on his job, they said I could then let him know
that his behavior had been inappropriate by gently embarrassing him in team
meetings. For example, I could say, "This week, since I made a special point to
look over your handouts . . . ," and so on. Following repeated embarrassments,
he would understand his actions had been misguided, they said.

On repeating these suggestions to some other American colleagues, they said
in horror: "That's not your job! What are you? His mother?"

For Americans, the T.A.'s behavior that cast me in a maternal and therefore
powerless role was bad enough. Why would I want to accentuate this image of a
weak woman boss? I should they said, instead restate my position as a boss, conveying to the T.A. my equal status with other bosses. The advice of the role-con-
scious Japanese was also intended to grant me the status of a boss, but it had to
be done within the context of a Japanese relationship of amae (sweetness). While
the American advice said, "Don't treat me as a mother/woman boss, and stand
up on your own feet," the Japanese advice said, "As your boss, I am telling you
that you need to work on your amae skills because it's costing others." Here was
another example of how Americans chose an explicit advice of independence
modeled on the working man, while the Japanese gave an implicit advice of interdependence modeled on the nurturing mother.

In the end, I decided to take a combined approach and called the T.A. into
my office. I told him that I had heard he thought I was treating him unfairly, and
that I had not intended to do so. Then I told him that the group was bearing the
cost of his behavior, and that although I would be happy to answer questions he
had on class preparation or marking, he really needed to shape up. The T.A. then
smiled from ear to ear, and said, "Thank you. I feel much better now that you
have scolded me." The problem was happily solved on all counts: The T.A. got
his solicited attention, the program was back on its feet, and I was on my way to
fulfilling my expected role as nurturer.

How It All Begins

Independent American decision makers and interdependent Japanese nurturers
don't just appear from nowhere. They are carefully socialized into becoming
players of their games through interaction first in the more private context of

their homes, and later in more public arenas of education, like schools. Linguist Patricia Clancy writes about Japanese children's education as mother-centered training.[4] In contrast, the American view sees the child as instrumental in her own learning; instead of talking about training or instruction, the child-centered perspective talks about acquisition, learning and development. Each philosophy plays a role in a child's socialization into the adult world, so that as the social psychologists William Caudhill and Helen Weinstein point out, different patterns of communication between American and Japanese children are already observable by as early as three to four months of age.[5]

In Japan, mothers see themselves as primarily responsible for their children's adjustment to mainstream society. Their lessons are not conscious but implicit, and include instruction on Listener Talk and interdependence. For example, the sociologist Ezra Vogel, in his study of mothers in a suburb of Tokyo, found that immediately after birth, mothers tried to ascertain the conditions under which their babies cried.[6] By minimizing the infant's vocalization, Japanese mothers begin to teach their infants not only about the value of silence, which is the backbone of Listener Talk, but also about the importance of sensing other's feelings in *amae* interdependence. Such "empathy training," as Patricia Clancy calls it, is continued throughout the years of a child's development. Communicating by example, the mother often steps into the shoes of the child to first show the desirable emotional reaction in an interdependent relationship of amae.

I saw an example of empathy training one afternoon in Hyde Park in London. A Japanese child, obviously cranky from the long day, launched an umbrella from his stroller like a javelin. He was delighted at the sight, but his mother was saddened: "Mama kanashii na. Kei-chan ii no ka na, mama kanashikute mo." (Mom's really hurt. Does Kei feel it's O.K. for mom to be so sad?)

A dog came by to sniff at the umbrella, and the mother added: "Hora wan-chan itteru yo. 'Kei-chan no kasa ga sasannakute, yokatta' tte." (See, listen to what the doggie's saying. 'I'm glad Kei's umbrella didn't stab me.')

This moral training in empathy contrasted with another scene I saw in an American supermarket. Instead of an umbrella, this time a boy is tossing cans of soup from his seat in the cart. The father scolds: "Hey come on! *Don't* throw the cans on the ground. Put them on the conveyor belt where they're supposed to be. The lady can't add them up if you don't put them on the conveyor belt. That's how you buy things. Put them on the conveyor belt."

Whereas the Japanese mother teaches her son about the interconnectedness of human emotions, the American child learns about individual logic: *If* you want to buy something, *then* put it on the conveyor belt. The message is direct and contrasts with the Japanese lesson, "Don't throw umbrellas because it could hurt someone," which is only implied through the reportedly sad feelings of the mother and the dog.

The Japanese lesson is also repeatedly taught by stand-in mothers who act as nurturers and disciplinarians. For example, in a similar supermarket scene, a

Japanese mother is in the purchasing aisle with her son who cannot see over the counter, but can reach the items on it. The boy has a toy in his hand, and with it, begins banging on the *ramen* (noodles) on the counter. His mother is involved in a conversation with another woman standing next to her, and doesn't notice it.

So the woman at the cash register stands in and says, "Aaaa. Ii no ka naaa. Boku." (O-Oh. I wonder if it's alright for me [male form] to do that). In standing in to cover for the boy's mother, the lady takes the position of the boy by using a male first person pronoun, "boku" (I). In the boy's voice, she says: Should I be doing this? What will mother think?

This question is echoed by the evil uncle lion in the recent Disney movie, "The Lion King" after he tricks the cub into thinking he has murdered his own father. Asking, "What will your mother think?" he reflects the origin of the story as the Japanese series, "Jungle Leo" (called "Simba" when aired in English), by the cartoonist Tezuka Osamu.

The lessons of Japanese empathy and American logic are further dovetailed by an education on Listener Talk and Speaker Talk. For example, Patricia Clancy describes an incident where a child called Maho is eating a plate and not her food. The mother uses metaphors of scary beasts and ghosts to imply that she is unhappy about Maho's behavior. The underlying message is that Maho should stop her bad behavior not because it is wrong, but because it is displeasing to her mother, which through empathy, should also be displeasing to Maho.

> MAHO'S MOM: *Kaijuu mitai. Kowai. Iya. Kowai, obake mitai. Mama obake kirai yo.* (Like a beast. It's scary. I don't like it. It's scary, like a ghost. I hate ghosts.)[7]

The implicit style of Maho's mother contrasts with the style used in the following excerpt by Kenny's mom. In a conversation recorded by a graduate student at the University of Arizona, Duane Boldt, Kenny's mother is similarly trying to get her son to focus on eating the food rather than playing with it. But her style is explicit, and her rationale is one of logic.

> KENNY'S MOM: No, you can't flick the—your food or throw it, you eat it. You don't play with it, it is not a toy. . . . It's food, you eat it.

While both mothers have the same short-term goal of wanting their children to eat their food, their approaches differ in how that goal is accomplished because each child must learn a different communicative game plan to survive in different adult worlds of Speaker Talk and Listener Talk. Such lessons are repeated time and time again as illustrated in the following two introductory courses on American "Individual Action Talk" and Japanese "Togetherness Talk."

One day in the D.C. suburbs, I had begun to eat my sandwich in the car when I noticed a Boy Scout and his mother setting up a stand outside a Block-buster Video shop. It turned out to be a popcorn stand, and the boy and his mother busily set about stacking the popcorn, and putting up the "$5.00/pack" sign. Taken by the moment, I decided to go up and buy one.

When I began my exchange for the purchase, I directed my request to buy the popcorn in the general direction across the stand. The mother, palm faced up, then began to gesture towards her son. I got the message, and asked for my popcorn again, this time exclusively addressing the Scout.

When my purchase was complete, I asked the boy whether he needed some tape for his sign. I had some tape in my car from sending off packages earlier that day, and I noticed his sign was flapping around, and in danger of being blown away. The boy appeared troubled by my question, and looked to his mother for help.

But to this she responded, "Honey, it's up to you. It's your decision."

Reflecting on this weighty piece of advice, the scout finally said, "I'll take it."

As we taped on the sign, I couldn't help but marvel at this early lesson in Individual Action Talk where the boy's mother, encouraging the scout to be on his own, looked suspiciously like a scout master.

An entirely different lesson is taught in a Japanese preschool. In her book, *Learning To Go To School In Japan,* Lois Peak identifies the role of a preschool teacher as critical to a child's mastery of *shuudan seikatsu* (life in a group).[8] As many as 99.6 percent of preschool teachers in Japan are women, which further reinforces the image and position of women as nurturers and shapers of Japan's future population.[9] In her extensive study of preschools in Nagano, Peak notes that preschool teachers play an important role in gradually weaning a child from the *amae* indulgence given at home to participate in the lessons of cooperative and collective behavior at school.

Several critical routines help accomplish this goal. The first is copying good behavior, or behavior-by-example. Because three-year-olds are thought to be too young to learn rules and procedures, instead, everyone is united by an implicit instruction to do things together. For example, the instruction "Everyone else is sitting down" invites children to sit down without actually commanding them to do so.[10] The undesirable prospect of being left out motivates a child to follow the group.

A second routine supports the first as it gets peers to echo good behavior. By encouraging group members to say for example, "Everyone is quiet," children, rather than the teacher, keep each other in line. A final strategy is to keep the children waiting until everyone is ready to carry out a task, move to the next activity, or partake in a ritual *aisatsu* (greeting). This again encourages pressure from the peers of noncompliant children as they silently signal, "Hurry up so we can get on to our next activity."

The younger the child is, the more individual attention he will need to carry out the routines, and this often takes the form of repetition where the teacher accomplishes her goals by outdoing the child in a game of perseverance, rather than by scolding. Here is an example illustrated in Lois Peak's translated transcription.[11]

TEACHER: Let's go into the classroom. Just for a few minutes. Let's go inside and say hello to Lord Buddha. Let's go into the classroom and all say good morning together.

[The teacher continues in this vein, approaching each child where he is playing. She comes to speak to Satoshi, who is playing with trucks in the sand.]

TEACHER: Let's go say good morning.

SATOSHI: Iya da. (I don't want to).

TEACHER: Let's go.

[The teacher tries to pick him up and carry him in, but Satoshi escapes and runs back to the toy trucks.]

SATOSHI: I still want to play.

TEACHER: You still want to play? Then play. Everyone's going inside. You can play. All by yourself. Okay? All by yourself. Goodbye.

After the teacher goes indoors to leave Satoshi on his own for a while, the director takes her place. She tells him he is a good boy, acknowledging only his good behavior. She then invites Satoshi in again.

Satoshi immediately rejects the invitation, so the director picks him up and brings him inside. He starts to kick and hit her, saying he still wants to play, but she pretends not to notice. At the entrance, when the director gives Satoshi his indoor shoes, he has more tantrums, throwing his shoes, and screaming "Iya da. Iya da" (I don't want to, I don't want to) all along. The director still continues to ignore him.

As the other students wait for Satoshi to take part in the morning greeting, the director bends her body over Satoshi's so that they bow together, and say, "Ohayoo gozaimasu" (good morning) with the others. Despite his tantrums, then, Satoshi is outdone because he ends up doing what he didn't want to do anyway. When the morning ritual is done, the director invites him back outside to play, but by this time Satoshi cannot even enjoy what he said he wanted to do earlier. Playing was only worth pursuing when it served as a contest to the will of authority. Now it was pointless. Repeated lessons of this nature teach Japanese children about the futility of going against collective interests, as well as about the rewards of pleasing others.

This desire to please bears a striking resemblance to a similar value allegedly inculcated in American women. But in the United States, this desire is seen more in terms of a weakness; it is what Oprah Winfrey calls "the disease to please." Women, who seek harmony and arbitrate conflict, shouldn't have to try to please the whole world, says this argument. They should be independent, stand up for themselves and do what they want. And, the most efficient instrument for achieving this desirable Equal Opportunity Independence is paid work. Such is the way American women define success today; they use the same rules American men have historically used to define the prestigious attributes which we now identify as professional.

In contrast, in the upper echelon of Japanese corporations is an executive-sage whose primary job is to provide company direction through establishing a corporate philosophy and a nurturing environment. The goal of such executives is to create an amae interdependence where there normally might not be one, and to recreate themselves as nurturing mothers who guide corporate members initially having *soto* (outside) relationships to participate in a corporate family. In business and in everyday life, the nurturing mother is the symbolic role model for the Japanese, while the working man is the metaphor of success for the Americans.

10

You Are What You Speak

The squeaky wheel gets the grease.

Tori mo nakaneba utaremaji.
(If the bird had not sung,
it would not have been shot.)

Some time ago I was at lunch with a Japanese friend, Keiko, when she began telling her Chinese American friend, Annie, and me a story about her roommate during college days in New England: "Theresa was building this image of herself as being *really* cosmopolitan," said Keiko. "But one day, her mother comes up to visit us, and says to me, 'Keiko, could you do me a favor, and say something for me in Chinese?'"

The story is all too familiar, and I burst out laughing, adding my own story: "That reminds me of the time I went to the supermarket and a lady asked me if I knew where the water chestnuts were!" Keiko and I howl together in laughter some more but Annie was clearly offended.

"If someone said something like that to me," she said, "I would just tell them straight out: 'I'm sorry, I'm American.'"

Neither Keiko nor I were American, so we could not have come back with Annie's retort. But her remark showed that there were at least two ways to be offended by the above examples of mistaken identities. For Keiko and me, the offense was about us as Japanese, being mistaken for Chinese. But for Annie, the offense was that anything Asian was being singled out at all; in so many words it was saying she was un-American.

The perceived insult was then, centered on different emphases in identity. For Keiko and me, the Japanese in the conversation, the mistaken identity was about who *we were not:* Because Japanese identity is constructed in part by drawing a distinction between the uchi (inside) group of *nihonjin* (Japanese) and the soto (outside) world of *gaijin* (foreigners), an offense can be made by mistaking the Japanese for the people from whom they want to distinguish themselves, like the Chinese. Characteristic of this desire for distinction is the Japanese term *Ajia-jin* (Asians), used to refer to all Asians but the Japanese themselves.

But for Annie, the American in the conversation, the mistaken identity was about who *she was:* Joining multicultural America means you are an American despite your origin, so pointing to an Asianness—Chinese or Japanese—tells the immigrant that she isn't quite American enough.

In reality, the distinction between the American and Japanese Asians in the conversation was not quite as straightforward. Both Keiko and I had spent enough time in the United States to understand Annie's point of view, and Annie, a third-generation Chinese American, could also see the offense in not seeing the distinction among Asians. What's more, in both the United States and Japan, some citizens strive earnestly and explicitly to meet the nation's ideals, while others knock them.

But in spite of the range of possible reactions, national ideals provide the context within which both supporters and protestors react. For example, sitting in a counter at a Starbucks cafe in Washington, D.C., I recently saw three bleached-blonde, teenage *shinjinrui* (the new generation) demonstrating a symbolic protest against the traditional image of the Japanese. "Gaijin ni naroo" (a fatalistic rendering of "(I'm) going to become a foreigner") said one of the three staring adoringly at a blonde woman sitting across from them. What the Japanese teenager did not realize was that her protest, intended to dispute a Japanese identity, only ended up giving further evidence for it because her use of the word *gaijin* (foreigner) refers to the Japanese division of the world into an inside group consisting of the Japanese, and an outside one of foreigners.

The Japanese/outsiders distinction is central to a Japanese identity, and blurring the division poses a threat to a Japanese definition of the world. I learned this once when I was working part-time in a Japanese company, and my co-workers expressed amazement at my ability to "make those special engine-sounding r-sounds—R-R-R—that only gaijin (foreigners) can make." They promptly concluded that both my height (I'm five-foot-seven and tall by Japanese standards) and ability to speak English were a result of eating American hamburgers in my formative years. It mattered little to them that my parents and grandparents were also tall—perhaps because, as the psychologist Kawai Hayao points out, a common unconscious belief is that we cannot return once we have eaten in another world.[1] But dietary habits outside, the logic of my Japanese co-workers was straight out of the guidebook for a Japanese identity: You are Japanese because you speak Japanese, and if you speak Japanese, you do not—indeed you cannot—speak a foreign language fluently.

What speaking Japanese is to a Japanese identity, American English is to an American identity. The difference is of course that unlike the proportionally small Korean and Chinese immigrant population of Japan, the United States has a relatively large influx of immigrants who bring with them their native languages. For these naturalized Americans, their American identity is made official not only by obtaining U.S. citizenship, but also by learning English. For example, when

I became an American citizen in 1993, my eligibility was considered under two criteria: a minimal knowledge of American history and an ability to speak English.

American English is key to an American identity. Take for example a full-page advertisement I saw in an in-flight magazine. On top of the page in bold letters was a message that read, "To Make It in America You Need to Speak My Language." Beneath this caption was a large photo of an Asian woman wearing a white lab coat embroidered with the letters: The Mount Sinai Hospital. Under the photo was her formal identity: Dr. Selina Chen-Kiang, Molecular Biologist. The text continued in Dr. Chen-Kiang's voice, "And today that language is English, even though I still speak Chinese at home. . . ." The ad finished by describing Dr. Chen-Kiang's unblemished academic record and her immigrant status in the United States. At the bottom was the identity of the distributor, U.S. English, a group that identifies itself as a national, non-partisan, non-profit organization that promotes English: the language of equal opportunity.

The message in the ad was clear: If you want to make it in America, speak English. And the logic was straightforward. English is not only the language of the founding fathers of America and the language in which the U.S. constitution is written, but also the language of the majority. American English is, in short, the vehicle for American unity—not only for the practical concerns of communication, but as a symbol of American identity. Speak whatever language you like at home, but to be American, speak English.

As linguistic ideals become part of our history and create the context for our actions, they have the potential to become a philosophy—a way of life—or, a self-fulfilling propaganda. But whichever way you look at it, Americans and Japanese both believe that you are what you speak. Language is the ultimate badge of national membership, and holding the official view awards a member a good citizenship standing. Because our views about our mother tongues affect the way we communicate, it is important that Americans and Japanese confront these views so that both sides can understand each other better by examining themselves. This concluding chapter, then, takes an introspective look at the American English and Japanese languages to explore how each is symbolic of its respective identity, and the effects such symbols have on the United States and Japan. To begin this final phase of uncovering American and Japanese communication, here are the folklores of each country, told in the way their citizens tell it.

In the Beginning

Once upon a time, a very long time ago, in the Plain of High Heaven were two deities, the sky-father, Izanagi, and the earth-mother, Izanami. The celestial team speared the seas to produce the islands that were to be called Japan, and spawned a host of other gods including the most famous, Amaterasu Oomikami, the Sun Goddess. For it was the Sun Goddess who was to send her grandson, Ninigi-no-

Mikoto to rule Japan, and it was Ninigi-no-Mikoto's great grandson that was to become enthroned as Japan's first recorded emperor of Shinto, The Way of the Gods.

In the first half of the millennium or so, political strife and civil unrest were rampant, and Japan was under constant threat from religious and intellectual invasion brought on by her neighboring countries—especially China. Japan grew in this context of pressures from the outside until Regent Shotoku wove foreign Buddhist, Confucian and Taoist principles together with native Shinto to form the seventeen articles that were later to become the first constitution of Japan.

From this locus, the Japanese civilization was born. Though feudal lords continued their territorial battles, and the ruling power oscillated wildly between the lords and the emperor, there was one thing that remained constant: the hostile threat from the outside. And from the Mongolians to the Russians, Japan withstood them all, incubating her native Yamato race by cleverly weaving together foreign borrowings, and making them her own. So much so that finally, even as an outsider forced the last Shinto emperor to denounce his godly status some fourteen centuries later, the Japanese were unified under a single sociopolitical ethic coded in a native language—Japanese—the symbol of shared interdependence that circles off the Japanese from the outsiders.

Now once upon another time, not too long ago, in a place called Spain, lived a King, Fernando, and his Queen, Ysabel, who gave her jewels to an Italian explorer named Columbus so that he could sail west and reach India in the east. The island he reached was part of what was to be called America.

In 1620, after several more landings on various shores of America, the first groups of settlers, called the Pilgrims, reached the harbor of Plymouth on their ship, the Mayflower. There, they signed a form that began:

> In the name of God, Amen. We whose names are underwritten, the loyal subjects of our dread sovereign Lord, King James, by the grace of God, of Great Britain, France, and Ireland king, defender of faith, etc., having undertaken for the glory of God, and advancement of the Christian faith, and honour of our king and country, a voyage to plant the first colony in the northern parts of Virginia. . . .[2]

Two and a half centuries and a civil war later, a statue erected in the New York Harbor enshrined the symbol of American freedom, inviting the tired, the poor and the huddled masses. And they came to America, first from the old country and then from every corner of the world, to pursue the American dream. And so the American civilization was founded on the shoulders of these immigrants, unified by a sociopolitical ethic coded in the native language—American English—once symbol of melting-pot unity, now symbol of unity in multiculturalism.

Every day, millions of Japanese and Americans reference these national legends to explain what makes the Japanese Japanese, and the Americans, American.

As autobiographical histories passed on from generation to generation, they are neither completely factual nor entirely true because history is selective, and an autobiography is an idealized perspective of a single viewpoint. As such, Americans and Japanese each describe their history from their own "perspective of the elephant"; being a part of the story means that there are parts—a leg, a trunk—that each cannot see. Laced in fiction, Americans and Japanese tell each other these stories to justify who they are, how they came to be, and what they need to become American and stay Japanese.

Becoming American, Staying Japanese

The traditional melting pot story goes like this. An immigrant arrives in the United States, and destitute though he might be, he has the chance to make it. Using every resource available, he does everything he can to obtain a piece of the American pie. If this involves learning another language, then so be it. Jump in the American melting pot, call out the Statue of Liberty and previous immigrants, speak English, and you too can be like one of us. The ideal melting-pot story is told by immigrants in a future voice of forecast: You too *can* become American by joining the pot of unity. Like the American army jingle, the positive message for the new immigrant is that he can "Be all that you can be" if he becomes American.

In contrast, the traditional Japanese story is told by the long-established native, who, though threatened by outsiders, is still Japanese. Despite heavy borrowing of Chinese (in particular its writing system), the Japanese language has remained separate and unrelated to the languages of the Asian mainland. The ideal Japanese story is told in a voice of history: We are Japanese because we have managed to stay Japanese, both in thinking and in language. A popular strategy for maintaining this self-perception has been to fan the foreign belief that the Japanese language is difficult to learn, and the Japanese culture, difficult to understand. For the greatest fear of a Japanese is the loss of language, because it is synonymous with the loss of a Japanese identity. Such a fear is made concrete by Japanese immigrants to the Americas: From the Japanese point of view, these Japanese emigres are no longer Japanese because they no longer speak Japanese.

The force of fear is reversed in the United States: If immigrants tell each other of the dire necessity to learn English, it is because of the fear of never gaining an American identity: Staying un-American means being divided forever. Responding to the current dilemma on how to manage multiculturalism, American English is the agreed upon answer: It represents national unity despite different peoples, religions and ideas. To be American is, then, to believe that unity can be achieved only if everyone speaks English, a contrastive view to the Japanese, who believe unity is achieved only if the Japanese speak Japanese.

The politics of these points of view on American English and Japanese creates a dynamics where speakers of American English seek to convert non-English speakers into their world of English, while speakers of Japanese try to keep these foreign-language speakers at an arm's length distance. Like an American who embraces a Japanese with open arms, and the Japanese who cringes and pulls away, the continuing trade friction is a classic example of this complementary schismogenesis. Applying every means possible, the United States tries to open up the "closed" Japanese markets, while the Japanese back off further, padding their organizations with "barbarian handlers" to keep foreigners at bay. Crossing their threshold of tolerance, the U.S. then finally serves up an ultimatum: Open up or else. . . . As the destructive playoff continues, neither is aware that what each is really battling is its own demon of cultural insecurity.

Mirror, Mirror

"What's PURE? Touch Me! *Motto chikaku e koi.* (Come closer.)" Thus screams a Japanese ad for PURE shampoo and rinse.[3] Running down the entire left side of the ad is a vertical trapezoid photo of a shoulder with shower water beating down on it; just above the shoulder is where it says, "Touch Me." Floating in the middle of the page is a photo of a cute-sexy girl-woman with a white bow in her hair. In the next sentence, the Chinese character for *koi* is a pun: The character used for *koi* is the one that means "love" instead of the verb "come." The more literal reading of this sentence using the pun might be something like, "Closer for love."

As in this ad where English makes up two-thirds of the big print, there is a remarkably high incidence of foreign word use in the Japanese mass media, which the sociolinguist Harald Haarmann calls a "playground for foreign language use."[4] This is particularly surprising in a nation where a reported 98 percent or more of its people are monolingual—they speak only Japanese. Why present an ad in a foreign language to monolinguals who constantly feel threatened by outsiders? Haarmann argues that English carries an aura of prestige for the Japanese; it has a ring of things modern and free. Advertisers use English to play up this emotional sale, promising buyers the privilege of the lifestyle invoked in the product.

So what's PURE? PURE isn't just a shampoo and rinse that washes your hair, PURE promises to make you pure—it will cleanse you of all unwanted foreign impurities. At the same time you can still buy the essence of the cute-sexy Eurasian girl-woman with wavy locks pictured in the oval photo. That is just an exotic fantasy; you are just buying a desire, but you can still stay Japanese. "Motto chikaku e koi"; come closer to buying your dream without cost.

PURE is an example of how Japanese manage their fear of losing their Japanese identity. Shower us with foreign words, it will just make us more Japanese, they say. Like the theatrical role of *hikitateyaku* (literally, the patronizing role) where a below-average character is intentionally placed on stage alongside the main character to make the star shine, exotic foreign-word use acts as a mirror that reflects Japanese uniqueness, making its form more definite. Like the *gaiatsu* (foreign pressure) applied in U.S.–Japan politics, foreign languages and policies act as the counter force that makes the Japanese more internally cohesive, defining them more clearly as insiders and foreigners as outsiders.

But all of this is possible only if the foreign language stays relatively superfluous—that is, it has to be used as an accessory. A common method employed by Japanese advertisers to achieve this is to combine foreign words in a silly and often nonsensical way. For example, I have a notebook on my table that has the following printed on the front cover:

TYRO SPIT BALLS? FOUL PLAY
10 BALKS A GAME!
Scandal, screwballs,
and the fans are angry
DIAMOND ABSURDITIES

Then on the back:

COPPEPANTS
I SIMPLY WANT TO STAND IN A
FARAWAY
LAZY
LAND

Definitely grammatical, and arguably imaginative, the English on this notebook does little in the way of harm. Rather, argues the applied linguist Takashi Kyoko, the English used in such ads aims to give a special effect, and has little concern for English grammar, or how it might come off sounding to an English-speaking audience.[5] The only care of advertisers is that it impart a Japanese interpretation of a carefree American lifestyle.

Another American clothes buyer had a similar experience: When she approached a Japanese clothing company to correct the mistakes printed on their clothing, they turned her away, saying that English was there just for the effect, and that it did not matter that the phrases were not "perfect" or "fluent." In fact, it mattered a great deal that the English was *not* perfect because fluency in English threatens the Japanese identity based on a Japanese/Gaijin (foreigner) distinction. Native fluency in English or another foreign language, unlike the use of foreign words as accessories, subtracts from a Japanese identity. Unfortunately for the Japanese company, their exclusive thinking, coupled with other market factors, led to the closing of the majority of their retail stores in the United States.

The Japanese use of a foreign language as a counter force also gives us an answer to the frequent question about why the Japanese have a difficult time learning English. The belief that the Japanese cannot be or speak anything but Japanese creates the defensive mechanism: We are unable to learn English. That is why a nation with six years of compulsory English is also 98 percent monolingual. The Japanese cannot learn English because it would undermine the very identity that defines who they are *not*. Failing at a foreign language is, then, a kind of proof that you are Japanese. But such a negative self-definition is costly not only in the market, but also in personal relationships since it hinders them from achieving amae interdependence and intimacy with Americans. By not learning foreign languages well, the Japanese forfeit the chance to really understand Americans even on their own terms.

Americans are subject to a similar handicap because English, heralded as the American language, is encouraged at the cost of immigrant and foreign languages. Reflecting this attitude, language programs are the first to go when universities suffer from budget cuts, and the United States is the only country in the world where you can get a Ph.D. without studying a foreign language.[6] In a country where plural languages pose the threat of segregation, English is seen as the unifying solution.

The Polish eye doctor Ludwig Zamenhof had a similar logic for creating an artificial language he called Esperanto. Like the U.S., Zamenhof himself was reportedly the host of many languages: He used Russian at home, Yiddish, Polish and Hebrew at the synagogue, and French, German, Latin, Greek and English in school. Not surprising then was Zamenhof's quest for a universal language, which together with a universal religion called Homoranismo, was crafted as a medium that would facilitate international communication and relations.

At one point Esperanto was somewhat successful, with some thirty-one thousand members reported to be in the World Esperanto Association (WEA) in 1979.[7] But at about the same time, WEA lost out to the advocates of another movement called English as an International Language (EIL) because: (1) Esperanto was an artificial language without native speakers, (2) Esperanto was created in the context of an unpopular political philosophy, communism and (3) economically well-to-do, English-speaking countries provided the financial backbone for EIL. These factors added up to make English a widely spoken language, boasting the top position among the world's official languages, and second only to Chinese in its number of native speakers.[8]

But it is also precisely this powerful position of English that has created an economics where learning about the English-speaking world has become a one-way street. For example, while all Japanese students begin studying English from middle school onwards, a mere 45,700 students, mostly at the university level, were studying Japanese in the U.S. in 1992.[9] Worse still is the enormous information gap that exists between the Japanese and the Americans. In 1990, the Japanese translated more than three thousand books written in English, but

Americans only translated and published eighty-two from Japanese.[10] The power of English has made the English-speaking world complacent, assuming that everything they need to know could be found in English, and never able to know otherwise.

Misunderstanding in cross-cultural communication often begins with a misunderstanding of ourselves. The possessiveness in the view that no one can speak Japanese but the Japanese, and the evangelism of the perspective that everyone should speak English are blind spots exposed only when compared to one another. It is then, for this comparison that the Americans and the Japanese need each other—a comparison which not only points out each other's shortcomings, but also creates the context for understanding each other's differences.

Inside Out

Despite the so-called shrinking world advocated and popularized by the media, the communication gap between the United States and Japan has remained unfilled, and United States–Japan relations have soured through incessant blaming. As neither side is able to get a handle on the origins or the reasons for the bad blood, mutual mistrust continues to fester because communicators in the throes of their misunderstanding are without the resources or skills for rectification.

By sharing my personal experiences and professional study of American and Japanese communication, I hope I have shown that there is a way out of the stalemate. The key, as I have argued throughout the book, is to try to understand American and Japanese communication and relationships in their own right—to see the Americans and the Japanese for who they really are. To understand Americans is to understand the explicit delivery of Speaker Talk: a gameplan that abides by the principle of Equal Opportunity Independence, in which an individual speaker takes the responsibility for articulating his or her message in as straightforward and honest as presentation as possible. And, to understand the Japanese is to understand the implicit goal of Listener Talk: A gameplan constructed on *amae* (sweetness) interdependence, where speakers distance talk so that listeners ultimately share in the responsibility of interpreting the unspoken messages of the interaction. This book has illustrated how these game plans are carried out in a range of communicative strategies, such as opening conversations and topics, making points, teasing, praising, telling the truth and showing support. Arguing that such differences arise as a result of different sets of ideals, I have also illustrated examples of differences between the interaction and communication of American and Japanese women (and men), and how such differences are passed on from generation to generation.

In comparing differences in American and Japanese behavior and communication, I have tried to maintain the integrity of each insider's perspective instead of interpreting all perspectives from a single viewpoint. Insider information will not close deals or magically sweeten cross-national relationships, but it can make each game more comprehensible, serving then to reduce the bewilderment and frustration that often accompany cross-cultural communication between Americans and Japanese. Like hands-on experience, insider information can supply the missing link to close the communication gap, and make the same problem more manageable. More important still, insider information opens up a whole new world that can help us not only to better understand ourselves, but also to hear the way we sound to our cross-cultural partners. It is not only comparison, then, but a comparison of the insider's perspectives that leads to the level of understanding necessary in cross-cultural communication.

Understanding Americans and Japanese is not a factual or objective study. The answer is to examine our own ways of interaction and communication in comparison to other cultures; the answer to understanding cross-cultural communication is inside out.

NOTES

Preface

1. In *Going International: How to Make Friends and Deal Effectively in the Global Marketplace.* (New York: Random House, 1985).

2. "The Big Split: Japan vs. the U.S." *Fortune,* May 6, 1991, 40.

3. "What Japan Thinks of Us: A Nation of Crybabies?" *Newsweek* April 2, 1990, 18–22, 24.

Chapter 1: Two Stories, Two Games

1. I have been told that a more literal translation of the original version exists in Japanese where the rejected grasshopper sadly walks away at the end of the story.

2. In *Nihonjin to Amerikajin: Koko ga oochigai.* (*Japanese and Americans: Here's the Big Difference*). (Tokyo: Bungei Shunju, 1985).

3. In *Japanese Patterns of Behavior.* (Honolulu, University of Hawaii Press, 1976), p. 40.

4. (New York, Warner Books, 1992).

5. In Jerry Greenwald, *Creative Intimacy: How to Break the Patterns That Poison Your Relationships.* (New York: Simon and Schuster, 1975), p. 13. I originally came across this in Livia Polanyi's book, *Telling the American Story: A Structural and Cultural Analysis of Conversational Storytelling.* (Cambridge, MA: MIT Press, 1989), p. 133.

6. For Doi's original work in Japanese, see *Amae no Koozoo* (*The Structure of "Amae"*). (Tokyo: Koobundoo, 1971). In English, *The Anatomy of Dependence.* Trans. by J. Bester. (Tokyo: Kodansha, 1973).

7. Uchiyama Kooshoo. *Opening the Hand of Thought: Approach to Zen.* Trans. Okumura Shoohaku and Tom Wright. Ed. Cary Warner. (New York: Penguin, 1993), p. 178. This is an excellent and readable introductory guide to Zen in English.

8. *Hitonami: Keeping up with the Satohs.* (Tokyo: Hakuhodo Institute of Life and Living, 1983).

9. Cheng, Chung-Ying, "Chinese Philosophy and Human Communication," in *Communication Theory: Eastern and Western Perspectives.* Ed. D. L. Kincaid. (San Diego, CA: Academic Press, 1987), p. 30.

10. Ohrbach, Barbara Milo. *All Things Are Possible: Pass the Word.* (New York: Clarkson Potter, 1995), p. 61.

11. See for example, the discussion in Lebra, Takie Sugiyama, *Japanese Patterns of Behavior* (5th edition). (Honolulu, HI: University of Hawaii Press, 1986).

12. In N. Namiki and S. P. Sethi's chapter on Japan, in R. Nath (ed.), *Comparative Management: A Regional View.* (Cambridge, MA: Ballinger, 1988), p. 57.

13. In *Crafting Selves: Power, Gender and Discourses of Identity in a Japanese Workplace.* (Chicago: University of Chicago Press, 1990).

14. In *Gender and Discourse.* (New York and Oxford: Oxford University Press, 1994), p. 25.

15. A comparison of *The Seven Samurai* and *The Magnificent Seven* also appears in Mizutani Osamu's book, *Nihongo no seitai.* (*Japanese: The Spoken Language in Japanese Life*). (Tokyo: Sotakusha, 1979).

16. In *Kotowaza ehon* (*Proverb Picture Book*). (Tokyo: Iwasaki Shoten, 1986).

17. In his article, "Inarticulateness," in *Linguistics in Context: Connecting Observation and Understanding.* Ed. Deborah Tannen. (Norwood, NJ: Ablex, 1988), pgs. 37–68.

The particular group of Native Americans McDermott discusses are the Menomeni Indians studied in the 20's by the well-known linguist, Leonard Bloomfield, and in the 60's by the equally well established sociolinguist, Dell Hymes.

It is also noteworthy that silence has been observed among other Native Americans (see for example, Philips's 1985 article on her study of Indians on the Warm Springs Reservation, and the Scollons' work with Athabaskans, 1981, 1985).

18. In Donal Carbaugh. *Talking American: Cultural Discourse on Donahue.* (Norwood, New Jersey: Ablex, 1988), pgs. 155–56.

19. This is my own translation, which is more literal than the one given in the film. The subtitles in the film are shown here: "This is the rule of war. Collective defense protects the individual. Individual defense destroys the individual."

20. Further explanation of Gregory Bateson's Double Bind Theory can be found in his *Mind and Nature: A Necessary Unity.* (New York: E. P. Dutton, 1979).

21. In Deborah Tannen's *That's Not What I Meant! How Conversational Style Makes or Breaks Relationships.* (New York: Ballantine Books, 1986), p. 17.

22. See *Crafting Selves: Power, Gender and Discourses of Identity in a Japanese Workplace.* (Chicago, IL: University of Chicago Press, 1990), for further description.

Chapter 2: Communication Equipment

1. In *A Reference Grammar of Japanese.* (New Haven: Yale University Press, 1975).

2. In Norbert Elias's translated book called *Time: An Essay,* published by Blackwell in 1992.

3. For a further discussion, see: *Language, Thought and Reality: Selected Writings of Benjamin Lee Whorf.* Ed. J. B. Carroll. (New York: Wiley, 1956).

4. In Elias, *Time: An Essay* (Oxford: Blackwell, 1992), p. 7.

5. A good book to read about this and the history of the English language is Jean Aitchison's *Language Change: Progress or Decay?* (2nd Edition) published by Cambridge, 1991.

6. This may be due to the more frequent use of *yaru* (give) to mean, "do."

7. In *Gender and Discourse.* (New York and Oxford: Oxford University Press, 1994), p. 26.

8. In *Discourse Strategies* (Cambridge: Cambridge University Press, 1982).

Chapter 3: Speak For Yourself, Listen to Others

1. In "The Perspective-Display Series and the Delivery and Receipt of Diagnostic News." In *Talk and Social Structure: Studies in Ethnomethodology and Conversation Analysis,* 164–92. Eds. Deidre Boden and Don H. Zimmerman. (Cambridge, MA: Polity Press, 1991).

2. Okazaki Shoko. *Ellipsis in Japanese Conversational Discourse.* Doctoral Dissertation. (Washington, D.C.: Georgetown University, 1994), p. 384.

3. There are more specific phone-answering rules, and I once got a booklet detailing exactly "How to answer a call." It included guidelines such as: (1) the maximum number of times for a phone to ring before it is picked up (three times, after that you should offer apologies); (2) the maximum time for a phone transfer (ten seconds); and (3) the maximum time for keeping a caller waiting (half a minute).

4. In *Metaphors We Live By,* published by the University of Chicago Press, 1980.

Chapter 4: Taking Care of Business

1. Mintzberg, quoted in Deirdre Boden's *The Business of Talk: Organizations in Action,* published by Polity Press, 1994, p. 51.

2. The transcripts of business conversations in the book are a mixture of examples that I overheard or were reported to me, and ones that I recorded, analyzed, and published in academic journals. The following guide lists the ten meetings from which they were extracted, together with the number of people involved and the national makeup of each group. To preserve anonymity and confidentiality, the names of the executives, financial institutions, accounts, and deals are changed.

Guide to Recorded Business Meetings

Meeting	Number of Members	Nationality
(1) Account Executives' Meeting	3	American
(2) Section Heads' Meeting	3	Japanese
(3) Personnel Meeting	2	1 American
		1 Japanese
(4) Corporate Banking Meeting	4	2 American
		2 Japanese
(5) Clients Research Meeting	5	Japanese
(6) CEO's Section Heads' Meeting	11	Japanese
(7) American Incentive Plan Meeting	2	American
(8) Cross-cultural Incentive Plan Meeting	2	1 American
		1 Japanese
(9) Risk-Based Capital Meeting	6	4 American
		2 Japanese
(10) Service Managers' Workshop	16	American

I recorded all meetings as they took place in their regular settings for an ongoing study of American/Japanese business communication. Transcriptions of (1) through (4) are of audio-recordings of meetings that took place in the summer of 1989; (5) through (10) are of video-recordings of meetings that took place in the summer of 1991. With the exception of (1), the Account Executives' Meeting, all were recorded at the same Japanese-owned bank in the United States. The Account Executives' Meeting (1) was recorded in another major American bank.

With the exception of (4) and (5), all meeting members are middle- to upper-middle managers with primary financial decision-making power. The exception in the Corporate Banking Meeting (4) is an office manager, Claire, whose supervisory breadth is limited to office administration. In the other exception, the Clients Research Meeting (5), a middle manager heads a group of junior members who only have secondary decision-making power.

3. In "Parenting in the late 90's," *New Roots,* 7(2): 1995, pgs. 1 and 11.

4. In Martin, Judith. "The Business of Being Polite." *The Washington Post,* April 15, 1990.

5. "The Cultural Premises of Japanese Diplomacy," in *The Silent Power,* edited by the Japan Center for International Exchange. (Tokyo: Simul Press, 1976).

6. In *Profiting from Education: Japan–United States International Educational Ventures in the 1980s.* (New York: Institute of International Education, 1990), p. 8.

7. In her analysis of the Japanese constitution, the linguist and historian Inoue Kyoko portrays the constitution as drafted as a tribute to MacArthur's notions of democracy. In *MacArthur's Japanese Constitution: A Linguistic and Cultural Study of Its Making.* (Chicago: The University of Chicago Press, 1991).

8. Reported in Edward T. Hall and Mildred Reed Hall's *Hidden Differences: Doing Business with the Japanese.* (New York: Anchor Press/Doubleday, 1987), p. 68.

9. In *Smithsonian,* January (1988): 145–56.

10. Taken from Michida Shinichiro. *Keiyaku-shakai: Amerika to nihon no chigai wo miru (Contractual Societies: Looking at Differences Between the United States and Japan).* (Tokyo: Yuhikaku, 1987).

Chapter 5: Open for Business

1 In *Eigo no hasso, nihon-go no hasso (English Expressions, Japanese Expressions).* (Tokyo: Nihon Hoso Shuppan Kyokai, 1992).

2. In *The Unspoken Way.* (Tokyo: Kodansha, 1988).

3. In "Opening Up Closings." (Expanded version). In *Language in Use,* ed. John Baugh and Joel Sherzer. (New York: Prentice Hall, 1982), 69–99.

4. In *Frame Analysis of a Japanese-American Contract Negotiation.* Doctoral Dissertation. (Washington, D.C.: Georgetown University, 1995).

5. In Michael Smitka's 1989, "Review of *Information, Incentives and Bargaining in the Japanese Economy* by Aoki Masahiko." *The Journal of Asian Studies* 48(4): 850.

6. In Takie Sugiyama Lebra's 1987 article, "The Cultural Significance of Silence in Japanese Communication." *Multilingua* 6(4): 344.

7. In Doi's article, "The Japanese Patterns of Communicating the Concept of Amae." In *Intercultural Communication: A Reader,* ed. Larry A. Samovar and Richard E. Porter. (Belmont, CA: Wadsworth, 1982), 220.

8. For comparisons of the more verbal with the less verbal, see, for example, Susan Philips's 1976 study of Anglo-American–Warm Springs Indian interaction; Ron Scollon and Suzanne B. K. Scollon's 1981 study of Anglo-American–Athabaskan Indian interaction; Deborah Tannen's 1981 and 1984 studies of New York Jewish–Californian conversation.

9. In Doi's article, "The Japanese Patterns of Communicating the Concept of Amae."

Chapter 6: Scoring Points

1. In *America and the Four Japans.* (Berkeley: Stone Bridge Press), 1994, p. 63.

2. For more on *ko-, so-, a-* words, see the Japanese linguist, Hosokawa Hirofumi's 1990 article, "Japanese Demonstratives Ko-, So-, and A-." In *The Georgetown Journal of Languages and Linguistics* 1(2): 169–78.

Chapter 7: Support Network

1. In S. Jameson and K. Schoenberger, "Japanese Find U.S. Workers a Puzzling Lot." Washington Post, August 11, 1988.

2. For example, see the following works:

Virginia LoCastro's 1987 study, "Aizuchi: A Japanese Conversational Routine." In *Discourse Across Cultures.* Ed. Larry E. Smith. (London: Prentice Hall), 101–113.

Senko Maynard's 1986 study, "On Back-Channel Behavior in Japanese and English Casual Conversation." *Linguistics,* 24: 85–114.

Mizutani Nobuko's 1982 study, "The Listener's Response in Japanese Conversation." *Sociolinguistic Newsletter,* 13(1): 33–38.

3. In *Language Crimes: The Use and Abuse of Language Evidence in the Courtroom.* (Cambridge: Blackwell, 1993), p. 8.

4. The term "turn-taking" was coined by the sociologists Harvey Sacks, Emanuel Schegloff and Gail Jefferson who wrote, "A Simplest Systematics for the Organization of Turn-Taking for Conversation," published in 1974 in *Language,* 50(4): 696–735.

5. See, for example, Frederick Erickson's 1982 study of Italian Americans: "Money Tree, Lasagna Bush, Salt and Pepper: Social Construction of Topical Cohesion in a Conversation among Italian-Americans." In *Analyzing Discourse: Text and Talk.* Georgetown University Round Table on Languages and Linguistics, ed. Deborah Tannen. (Washington, D.C., Georgetown University Press), 43-70.

Also see, Deborah Tannen's 1984 book, *Conversational Style: Analyzing Talk Among Friends* (Norwood, NJ: Ablex).

Deborah Tannen's 1994 chapter called "Interpreting Interruption" in her *Gender and Discourse* is also relevant.

Chapter 8: Teasing, Praising, and Repeating

1. In *You Just Don't Understand.* (New York: Simon and Schuster, 1990).
2. In *Gender and Discourse.* (New York: Oxford University Press, 1994).
3. In *Black and White: Styles in Conflict.* (Chicago: University of Chicago Press, 1981).
4. For a detailed analysis of a Japanese politician's rhetorical style, see, Senko K. Maynard's 1994 article "Image of Involvement and Integrity: Rhetorical Style of a Japanese Politician." *Discourse & Society,* 5(2): 233–61.
5. Gregory Bateson. *Steps to an Ecology of Mind.* (New York: Ballantine, 1972).

Chapter 9: Role Models

1. In *You Just Don't Understand: Women and Men in Conversation* (New York: William and Morrow, 1990), and *Talking From 9 to 5* (New York: William and Morrow, 1994).
2. Dallas: Spring Publications, 1988.
3. See *You Just Don't Understand: Women and Men in Conversation* (New York: William and Morrow, 1990).
4. In "The Acquisition of Communicative Style in Japanese." In *Language Socialization Across Cultures,* ed. Bambi B. Schieffelin and Elinor Ochs. (Cambridge: Cambridge University Press, 1986), 213–50.
5. In "Maternal Care and Infant Behavior in Japan and America." In *Japanese Culture and Behavior: Selected Readings,* ed. Takie Sugiyama Lebra and William P. Lebra. (Honolulu: University of Hawaii Press, 1986), 202.
6. In *Japan's New Middle Class: The Salary Man and His Family in a Tokyo Suburb.* (Berkeley: University of California Press, 1963).
7. In Patricia Clancy's 1986 article "The Acquisition of Communicative Style in Japanese." In *Language Socialization Across Cultures,* ed. Bambi B. Schieffelin and Elinor Ochs. (Cambridge: Cambridge University Press, 1986), 237. In her original translation, Clancy translates *obake* as monsters.
8. Berkeley: University of California Press, 1986.
9. Monbushoo (The Ministry of Education, Science and Culture) *Yoochien kyooiku no arikata ni tsuite.* (*The State of Preschool Education*). Tokyo: Monbushoo, 1986.
10. In *Learning to Go to School in Japan,* p. 130.
11. In *Learning to Go to School in Japan,* p. 175. I have changed the organization slightly from Lois Peak's original presentation. For example, when available, I put the Japanese text before the English because it is the primary text, rather than use the original format of English, then Japanese.

Chapter 10: You Are What You Speak

1. In *The Japanese Psyche: Major Motifs in the Fairy Tales of Japan.* (Dallas, Texas: Spring Publications, 1988), p. 102.

2. William Bradford's "History of Plymouth Plantation" (written 1630–51), 1898; book 1, ch. 9. In *The Faber Book of America,* ed. Christopher Ricks and William L. Vance. (London, Boston: Faber and Faber, 1994), p. 15.

3. In Harald Haarmann, *Symbolic Values of Foreign Language Use: From the Japanese Case to a General Sociolinguistic Perspective.* (New York: Mouton de Gruyter, 1989), p. 72.

4. In *Symbolic Values of Foreign Language Use: From the Japanese Case to a General Sociolinguistic Perspective.* (New York: Mouton de Gruyter, 1989), p. viii.

5. "Language and Desired Identity in Contemporary Japan." *Journal of Asian Pacific Communication,* 3(1) (1992): 133–44.

6. In Frederik L. Schodt, *America and the Four Japans.* (Berkeley, CA: Stony Bridge Press, 1994).

7. In David Crystal, *The Cambridge Encyclopedia of Language.* (Cambridge: Cambridge University Press, 1987), p. 354.

8. In David Crystal, *The Cambridge Encyclopedia of Language.* (Cambridge: Cambridge University Press, 1987), p. 287.

9. In "American Culture Told in Numbers," *San Francisco Chronicle,* November 2, 1992, p. A6.

10. In T. R. Reid, "Japan Opens a New Chapter on Exports," *International Herald Tribune,* August 29–30, 1992, and Richard J. Samuels, "Facing Japan as a Technological Superpower," *MIT Japan Science and Technology Newsletter,* January 1993, p. 2.

REFERENCES

Aitchison, Jean. 1991. *Language Change: Progress or Decay.* (2nd Edition). Cambridge: Cambridge University Press.

Bateson, Gregory. 1972. *Steps to an Ecology of Mind.* New York: Ballantine.

———. 1979. *Mind and Nature: A Necessary Unity.* New York: E. P. Dutton.

Benton, D.A. 1992. *Lions Don't Need to Roar: Using the Leadership Power of Presence to Stand Out.* New York: Warner Books.

Boden, Deirdre. 1994. *The Business of Talk: Organizations in Action.* Cambridge, MA: Polity Press.

Borboa, Roman A. 1995. "Parenting in the Late 90's," *New Roots,* 7(2).

Brislin, Richard and Yoshida, Tomoko. 1994. *Intercultural Communication Training: An Introduction.* Thousand Oaks, CA: Sage.

Brown, Douglas H. 1987. *Principles of Language Learning and Teaching.* Englewood Cliffs, NJ: Prentice-Hall.

Brown, Penelope, and Stephen C. Levinson. 1987. *Politeness: Some Universals in Language Usage.* Cambridge: Cambridge University Press.

Carbaugh, Donal. 1988. *Talking American: Cultural Discourse on Donahue.* Norwood, NJ: Ablex.

Caudhill, William and Helen Weinstein. 1986. "Maternal Care and Infant Behavior in Japan and America." In *Japanese Culture and Behavior: Selected Readings,* ed. Takie Sugiyama Lebra and William P. Lebra, 201–46. Honolulu: University of Hawaii Press.

Chambers, G. S. and W. K. Cummings. 1990. *Profiting from Education: Japan–United States International Educational Ventures in the 1980s.* New York: Institute of International Education.

Cheng, Chung-Ying. 1987. "Chinese Philosophy and Human Communication," in *Communication Theory: Eastern and Western Perspectives,* ed. D. L. Kincaid, 23–44. San Diego, CA: Academic Press.

Clancy, Patricia. 1986. "The Acquisition of Communicative Style in Japanese." In *Language Socialization Across Cultures,* ed. Bambi B. Schieffelin and Elinor Ochs, 213–50. Cambridge, MA: Cambridge University Press.

Copeland, L. and L. Griggs. 1985. *Going International: How to Make Friends and Deal Effectively in the Global Marketplace.* New York: Random House.

Crystal, David. 1987. *The Cambridge Encyclopedia of Language.* Cambridge: Cambridge University Press.

Doi Takeo. 1971. *Amae no koozoo (The Structure of "Amae")*. Tokyo: Koobundoo.

———. 1973. *The Anatomy of Dependence*. Translated by J. Bester. Tokyo: Kodansha.

———. 1982. "The Japanese Patterns of Communicating the Concept of Amae." In *Intercultural Communication: A Reader,* ed. Larry A. Samovar and Richard E. Porter, 218–22. Belmont, CA: Wadsworth.

Elias, Norbert. 1992. *Time: An Essay*. Oxford: Blackwell.

Erickson, Frederick. 1976. "Gatekeeping Encounters: A Social Selection Process." In *Anthropology and the Public Interest,* ed. Peggy Reeves Sanday, 111–45. New York: Academic Press.

———. 1982. "Money Tree, Lasagna Bush, Salt and Pepper: Social Construction of Topical Cohesion in a Conversation Among Italian-Americans." In *Analyzing Discourse: Text and Talk, Georgetown University Round Table on Languages and Linguistics 1981 ed.* Deborah Tannen, 43–70. Washington, D.C.: Georgetown University Press.

Fujiwara Mariko. 1983. *Hitonami: Keeping Up With the Satohs*. Tokyo: Hakohodo Institute of Life and Living.

Gardner, Robert C. and Wallace E. Lambert. 1972. *Attitudes and Motivation in Second Language Learning*. Rowley, MA: Newbury House Publishers.

Gomi Taro. 1986. *Kotowaza ehon (Proverb Picture Book)*. Tokyo: Iwasaki Shoten.

Greenwald, Jerry. 1975. *Creative Intimacy: How to Break the Patterns That Poison Your Relationships*. New York: Simon and Schuster.

Graham, John L. and Yoshihiro Sano. 1984. *Smart Bargaining: Doing Business with the Japanese*. Cambridge, MA: Ballinger.

Gumperz, John J. 1982. *Discourse Strategies*. Cambridge: Cambridge University Press.

Haarmann, Harald. 1989. *Symbolic Values of Foreign Language Use: From the Japanese Case to a General Sociolinguistic Perspective*. New York: Mouton de Gruyter.

Hall, Edward T. and Mildred Reed Hall. 1987. *Hidden Differences: Doing Business with the Japanese*. New York: Anchor Press/Doubleday.

Hosokawa, Hirofumi. 1990. "Japanese Demonstratives Ko-, So-, and A-." *The Georgetown Journal of Languages and Linguistics* 1(2): 169–78.

Inoue, Kyoko. 1991. *MacArthur's Japanese Constitution: A Linguistic and Cultural Study of Its Making*. Chicago: University Press of Chicago.

Jameson, S. and K. Schoenberger. 1988. "Japanese Find U.S. Workers a Puzzling Lot." *Washington Post,* August 11.

Kawai Hayao. 1988. *The Japanese Psyche: Major Motifs in the Fairy Tales of Japan*. Dallas: Spring Publications.

Kincaid, D. Lawrence, ed. 1987. *Communication Theory: Eastern and Western Perspectives*. San Diego, CA: Academic Press.

Kochman, Thomas. 1981. *Black and White: Styles in Conflict*. Chicago: University of Chicago Press.

Kondo, Dorinne K. 1990. *Crafting Selves: Power, Gender and Discourses of Identity in a Japanese Workplace*. Chicago: University of Chicago Press, .

Lakoff, George and Mark Johnson. 1980. *Metaphors We Live By*. Chicago: University of Chicago Press.

Lebra, Takie Sugiyama. 1986. *Japanese Patterns of Behavior* (5th Edition). Honolulu: University of Hawaii Press.

———. 1987. "The Cultural Significance of Silence in Japanese Communication." *Multilingua* 6(4): 343–57.

LoCastro, Virginia. 1987. "Aizuchi: A Japanese Conversational Routine." In *Discourse Across Cultures,* ed. Larry E. Smith, 101–13. London: Prentice Hall.

Martin, Judith. 1990. "The Business of Being Polite." *The Washington Post,* April 15.

Martin, Samuel. 1975. *A Reference Grammar of Japanese.* New Haven: Yale University Press.

Matsumoto Michihiro. 1988. *The Unspoken Way.* Tokyo: Kodansha, .

Maynard, Douglas 1991. "The Perspective-Display Series and the Delivery and Receipt of Diagnositc News." In *Talk and Social Structure: Studies in Ethnomethodology and Conversation Analysis,* eds. Deirdre Boden and Don H. Zimmerman, 164–92. Cambridge, MA: Polity Press.

Maynard, Senko. 1986. "On Back-Channel Behavior in Japanese and English Casual Conversation." *Linguistics* 24: 85–114.

———. 1994. "Image of Involvement and Integrity: Rhetorical Style of a Japanese Politician." *Discourse & Society,* 5(2): 233–61.

McDermott, R. P. 1988. "Inarticulateness." In *Linguisics in Context: Connecting Observation and Understanding,* ed. Deborah Tannen, 37–68. Norwood, NJ: Ablex.

Michida Shinichiro. 1987. *Keiyaku-shakai: Amerika to nihon no chigai wo miru (Contractual Societies: Looking at Differences Between the United States and Japan).* Tokyo: Yuhikaku.

Mizutani, Nobuko. 1982. "The Listener's Response in Japanese Conversation." *Sociolinguistic Newletter,* 13(1): 33–38.

Mizutani Osamu. 1979. *Nihongo no seitai (Japanese: The Spoken Language in Japanese Life).* Tokyo: Sotakusha.

Monbushoo (Japanese Ministry of Education, Science, and Culture). 1986. *Yoochien kiyooiku no arikata ni tsuite (The State of Preschool Education).* Tokyo: Monbushoo.

Mushakooji, Kinhide. 1976. "The Cultural Premises of Japanese Diplomacy." In *The Silent Power,* ed. The Japan Center for International Exchange. Tokyo: Simul Press.

Nakano, Yoshiko. 1995. *Frame Analysis of a Japanese-American Contract Negotiation.* Doctoral Dissertation. Washington, D.C.: Georgetown University.

Namiki, N., and Sethi, S. P. 1988. "Japan." In *Comparative Management: A Regional View,* ed. R. Nath, 55–96. Cambridge, MA: Ballinger.

Ohrbach, Barbara Milo. 1995. *All Things Are Possible: Pass the Word.* New York: Clarkson Potter.

Okazaki Shoko. 1994. *Ellipsis in Japanese Conversational Discourse.* Doctoral Dissertation. Washington, D.C.: Georgetown University.

Peak, Lois. 1991. *Learning to Go to School in Japan: The Transitionn From Home to Preschool Life.* Berkeley: University of California Press.

Pfeiffer, John. 1988. "How Not to Lose the Trade Wars by Cultural Gaffes." *Smithsonian,* January: 145–56.

Philips, Susan. 1976. "Some Sources of Cultural Variability in the Regulation of Talk." *Language in Society* 5: 81–95.

———. 1985. "Interaction Structured Through Talk and Interaction Structured Through Silence." In *Perspectives on Silence,* ed. Deborah Tannen and Muriel Saville-Troike, 205–214. Norwood, NJ: Ablex

Polanyi, Livia. 1989. *Telling the American story: A Structural and Cultural Analysis of Conversational Storytelling.* Cambridge, MA: MIT Press.

Powell, Bill and Bradley Martin. 1990. "What Japan Thinks of Us." *Newsweek,* April 2.

Rapoport, Carla. 1991. "The Big Split: Japan vs. the U.S." *Fortune,* May 6.

Reid, T. R. 1992. "Japan Opens a New Chapter on Exports." *International Herald Tribune,* 29–30 August.

Ricks, Christopher and William L.Vance. 1994. *The Faber Book of America.* London, Boston: Faber and Faber.

Sacks, Harvey, Emanuel Schegloff and Gail Jefferson. 1974. "A Simplest Systematics for the Organization of Turn-Taking for Conversation." *Language,* 50(4): 696–735.

Sacks, Oliver. 1985. *The Man Who Mistook His Wife for a Hat.* London: Pan Books. New York: Summit.

Samuels, Richard J. 1993. "Facing Japan as a Technological Superpower." *MIT Japan Science and Technology Newsletter,* January.

San Francisco Chronicle. "American Culture Told in Numbers," November 2.

Schegloff, Emanuel and Harvey Sacks. 1982. "Opening Up Closings." (Expanded version). In *Language in Use,* ed. John Baugh and Joel Sherzer, 69–99. New York: Prentice Hall.

Schiffrin, Deborah. 1987. *Discourse Markers.* Cambridge: Cambridge University Press.

Schodt, Frederik L. 1994. *America and the Four Japans.* Berkeley: Stone Bridge Press.

Scollon, Ron 1985. "The Machine Stops: Silence in the Metaphor of Malfunction." In *Perspectives on Silence,* ed. Deborah Tannen and Muriel Saville-Trorke, 21–30. Norwood, NJ: Ablex.

Scollon, Ron and Suzanne B. K. Scollon 1981. *Narrative, Literacy and Face in Interethnic Communication.* Norwood, NJ: Ablex.

Shuy, Roger W. 1993. *Language Crimes: The Use and Abuse of Language Evidence in the Courtroom.* Oxford and Cambridge MA: Blackwell.

Singleton, David. 1989. *Language Acquisition: The Age Factor.* Clevedon: Bristol, Avon, UK Multilingual Matters.

Smitka, Michael. 1989. "Review of *Information, Incentives and Bargaining in the Japanese Economy* by Aoki Masahiko." *The Journal of Asian Studies,* 48(4): 849–50.

Takashi Kyoko. 1992. "Language and Desired Identity in Contemporary Japan." *Journal of Asian Pacific Communication,* 3(1): 133–44.

Tannen, Deborah. 1981. "The Machine-Gun Question: An Example of Conversational Style." *Journal of Pragmatics,* 5: 5383–97.

———. 1984. *Conversational Style: Analyzing Talk Among Friends.* Norwood, NJ: Ablex.

———. 1986. *That's Not What I Meant! How Conversational Style Makes or Breaks Relationships.* New York: Ballantine Books.

———. 1990. *You Just Don't Understand.* New York: Ballantine.

———. 1994. *Talking From 9 to 5.* New York: Avon.

———. 1994. *Gender and Discourse.* Oxford: Oxford University Press.

Toyama Shigehiko. 1992. *Eigo no hasso, nihon-go no hasso (English Expressions, Japanese Expressions).* Tokyo: Nihon Hoso Shuppan Kyokai.

Tyler, Royall, ed. 1987. *Japanese Tales.* New York: Pantheon Books.

Vogel, Ezra. 1963. *Japan's New Middle Class: The Salary Man and His Family in a Tokyo Suburb.* Berkeley: University of California Press.

Wagatsuma Hiroshi. 1985. *Nihonjin to Amerikajin: Koko ga oochigai. (Japanese and Americans: Here's the Big Difference)*.Tokyo: Bungei Shunju.

Whorf, Benjamin Lee. 1956. *Language, Thought and Reality: Selected Writings of Benjamin Lee Whorf,* ed. J. B. Carroll. New York: Wiley.

Yamada, Haru. 1992. *American and Japanese Business Discourse: A Comparison of Interactional Styles.* Norwood, NJ: Ablex.

INDEX